Mountain Lion Rises

A MEMOIR OF HEALING

JACINTA HART KEHOE

Jacinta Hart Kehoe

Praise for Jacinta Hart Kehoe

MOUNTAIN LION RISES

"In this beautifully written memoir-in-essays, Jacinta Hart Kehoe offers a moving, clear-eyed account of family struggles, pain, loss, and ultimately, a courageous self-reckoning that sets her free and invites new love into her life. *Mountain Lion Rises* is gritty, poignant, inspiring, and bold."

—**Ann McCutchan**, author of six books, most recently, *The Life She Wished to Live: A Biography of Marjorie Kinnan Rawlings*. ann@annmccutchan.com

"Jacinta Hart Kehoe is a masterful writer. In lucid prose she gives us an unflinching, vivid account of the devastating tragedy that changed her life, and how, sustained by the companionship of friends, family, her animals, and the beauty of the natural world, she was able to move on and find happiness. A treasure."

—**Elizabeth Stuckey-French** is author of *The Revenge of the Radioactive Lady, Wicked, Mermaids on the Moon,* and *The First Papergirl in Red Oak, Iowa.*

"*Mountain Lion Rising* is an intense account of the redemptive nature of the world around us—if we have the patience and compassion to comprehend it. Jacinta Hart Kehoe has this patience and compassion and is able to translate it to the page gracefully in a difficult, honest, and hopeful story that is well worth the read."

—**BK Loren** is the author of many articles in literary and environmental magazines and several books: *The Way of the River: Adventures* *and Meditations of a Woman Martial Artist; Animal, Mineral, Radical: Essays on Wildlife, Family and Food;* and *Theft: A Novel.*

"The writer of a family memoir inherits certain advantages. She recalls events from life itself, and if she has the emotion and the skill required to write her story, she will give the reader a narrative that others often cannot. Jacinta Hart Kehoe has both the recollections and the literary qualifications required to write *Mountain Lion Rises...* And as we progress from the first page to the end, I'm repeatedly impressed by how unpredictable each chapter of this memoir is."

—**Patrick Irelan** is author of *Central Standard: A Time, a Place, a Family; Orchestrated Murder: An Iowa Murder Mystery; Reruns; The Miracle Boy; The Big Drugstore;* and *A Firefly in the Night.*

Two essays in this book previously appeared in the following publications:

The Examined Life: A Literary Journal of the University of Iowa Carver College of Medicine: "Salt River." 2012.

Good Housekeeping/SheBooks: "Coyote Tales." In "Every Mother has a Story." 2014.

Cover illustration: Jacinta Hart Kehoe

Cover design: Lucy Arnold

Typesetting: Christine Baker

ISBN 978-1-950251-12-4 (paperback)

ISBN 978-1-950251-14-8 (hardcover)

ISBN 978-1-950251-13-1 (Ebook)

Library of Congress Control Number: 2022922529

First edition

Printed in the United States of America

Published by:

National League of American Pen Women, Inc.

PEN WOMEN PRESS

Founded in 1897, the National League of American Pen Women, Inc.

is a nonprofit dedicated to promoting the arts.

1300 17th Street NW, Washington, D.C. 20036-1973

www.nlapw.org

For those who cherish life.

In Memory of Raymond

"There is a great deal of pity and tenderness in all of us, but when a certain balance is broken by things that create exhaustion, I think the underground devils come out —which makes for naked and savage kinds of creation."

Tennessee Williams
(A letter to Mary Hunter, 1943)

CHAPTER
One

SALT RIVER

Blue sky. Movement.

Flat on my back, I look straight up to a person who leans toward me.

"What happened?" I ask.

"We're putting you in an ambulance. You've been in an accident."

I feel tugs on my clothing.

"We have to cut your clothes off. You have to stay awake. Talk to me. Keep talking to me. Tell me anything you want to," the person commands.

Sometimes, I'm awake. Sometimes, I'm not sure. I repeatedly ask for news of my son, Raymond, my daughter, Elizabeth, and my husband, Jon. The answer is always the same, "There isn't news yet."

I think of my dog, Sasha, thinking that he was in the back of the van, that we lost him. Thinking of losing him makes me so sad. Then my mind fights itself, knowing that this isn't quite true as Sasha wasn't with us. Then, I have to think and think, force my brain to free itself from some huge blackness. I ponder about what I'm doing here. How I got here... the thoughts spin and churn, and I remember Raymond.

"Is my son okay?"

"We don't know yet."

"My husband?"

"Don't know yet."

"My daughter?" I know Elizabeth made it, but where is she? What happened to her? What did they do with her?

"Your daughter is okay."

Hearing that, I know the real answer about Jon and Raymond.

Still, I say over and over on the ride to the University of Iowa Hospitals and Clinics, "How is my daughter? Son? Husband?"

Now, I'm on a gurney being wheeled. Voices talk, excited. Voices command directions. I sleep. I wake. I sleep. Each time I awake, I ask, "My family, are they okay?"

It's always the same answer, not to worry, they are fine.

Two young women are now guiding the gurney. In their voices, I detect disgust and frustration about the lack of organization and competence, and why this family had to wait for so long. I put together that they are discussing things that have been done, or not done, in taking care of my family. I continue to doze.

I awaken as I am being moved from a soft surface to a hard one. I'm now aware that I am wearing a neck brace. Next, I'm rolled headfirst into a tunnel, which I later realize was for an MRI scan.

"Hold still," a voice echoes.

I fall back asleep.

"You held perfectly still," someone says as I'm being rolled out of the large machine.

"Can I sleep now?"

The same person responds, "Yes."

It is later now and a person leans over the railing of my bed.

I say, "You've got to call someone. I have animals that need to be taken care of."

I'm vaguely aware that much time has passed. I have no idea how long. I'm also aware that my speech is slow and slurred.

Names and faces spin like a roulette wheel in my head. I try to find the right one, a friend who can call others and who will know what to do. Who can get here fast? I must get out of here.

"Jan," I say. "Call Jan." She lives not far from the hospital and her phone number, which I say out loud, flashes in my head.

More time has passed and through the bed railings, I see a female figure in a white jacket pull up a chair and sit down. Her face is not visible. She says, "I have good news and bad news. This is the good news: your daughter is fine. This is the bad news: your husband and son are dead." And, then she is gone.

I try to move in answer and realize that I am strapped in. I believe her but I cannot grasp the immensity of what she has said, though I know in my heart that it is true.

Medical Records 12/14/03:... cyst in segment 4 of the liver. Posteriorly, there is a subcapsular fluid collection in segment 6 of the liver...

"Your liver was lacerated, didn't you know? You had to stay still for four days. If the liver didn't bleed again during that time, then you wouldn't have to have surgery. You would no longer be in danger of dying," a friend will tell me weeks later.

The Iowa Highway Patrol troopers come and peer at me. They talk as though I'm not there. They give their condolences and explain that they will interview me another time.

After a while a woman stands at the end of my bed. She reminds me of Jan. I will find out later that the nurses called Jan and she did come to my bedside.

Later I awake and find Elizabeth's violin teacher, Gwen, standing over my bed. I blurt out, "Gwen, Jon and Raymond didn't make it. I didn't get to die; I still have too much to learn."

I now remember that en route to Elizabeth's and Raymond's violin and piano recitals, there was a traffic jam on I-80 and our van ended up last in the long line. Gwen's appearance at my bedside begins to instigate recollections.

My mind sets off a recall of the atrocity. I hear the unmistakable sound of semi-truck brakes roaring from behind us. My legs dance and an instinctive desire to flee consumes me. I want to move the van, though I am not in control. In hopes of easing the intense apprehension, I blurt out, "Good thing he's putting on his brakes."

But Jon, with a sober expression, intently watches the rearview mirror.

Two years later, in a therapy session with Elizabeth, she will tell me, "Right before it hit, you turned around, Mom, and yelled, 'Watch OUT!'"

The Cahills lean over my bed. They are friends from church. Rosalie says, "We're trying to reach Father Ed."

I try to sit up, to acknowledge Rosalie and Jim and I want to look at my wrist. This urge evokes more memories.

In my mind, I hear Elizabeth crying. I open my eyes. My wrist hurts. It's slit open, the skin peeled back like a filleted fish. Blood drips from it. To my left, Jon's head is slung toward me. His body crumpled in the driver's seat, his hands thrown open as if grasping for something. I turn my head enough to see that Raymond is unnaturally bent over at the waist. Limp. Directly behind him, there is no van. The air blows in.

"We'll be okay," I say to Elizabeth, or maybe I think it. I'm in someone else's movie where time has slowed. Somehow, I know that Raymond has left this world. *I'll deal with it later. Maybe help will come.* I return to sleep.

"My animals. I've got to go home and take care of Elizabeth and my animals," I say aloud.

A voice answers, "They're being taken care of."

"I've got to go home. I've got to drive to Des Moines in the morning for my job. I'm getting out of here in the morning," I say to the woman who looks like my friend Jan.

Twice a month, I drove long distance on I-80 to attend meetings for my job. Due to the many gruesome accidents that I witnessed on these journeys, I preferred not to take my children on this route. Jon, however, refused to consider going other ways. He thought I worried too much.

———

Elizabeth is by my bed. Standing? Sitting?

"Tell her," Mary, my sister says. "It has to come from you."

I don't physically feel as though I'm in a bed. My body feels as though it has departed, leaving a mind and a voice that work intermittently.

"Give me your hand, Elizabeth." I take the hand that she has held out. I want to come out from deep within, to abandon this torpor, but it presses on me like a pillow of suffocation.

"I'm sorry, sweetie. I'm sorry." I want to reach her, reach inside of her, fix her. "Dad and Raymond didn't make it. They died," I say from my supine position. The words come out sounding counterfeit. I can't see her face. I can't be with her. Someone else should hug her.

"I didn't believe you," Elizabeth tells me two years later. "I thought you were lying to me and I hated you for it."

As kids do, she and Raymond argued before we left home over who should sit where in the van. "You two will always have each other, so be nice," I said and commanded that they choose a seat and stay put. They changed seats.

———

"How are you feeling?" The doctor asks.

"Like I'm about to vomit," I say as I begin to heave, which is painful with broken ribs.

She takes the bedpan from the counter and begins to walk toward me. As she approaches, bile starts to come out. The pan flies into my lap and out of the corner of my eye, I notice that the doctor is standing with her back towards me.

Medical Records 12/15/03:... She has been making slow but steady progress. Yesterday she had some vomiting. She has not had any today but has had some slight nausea...

"You've got to hold as still as possible," a male voice says from behind me. Two more medical personnel are also present. One holds down my legs, the other holds my shoulder. Whatever they are doing to my left side hurts so damn bad, I'd kill them if I had the energy. But I have no energy. I have no will to move.

"Ouch. Ow. Ow."

One of the men says with an incredulous voice, "That's all you have to say?"

Medical Records 12/15/03:... a 28-in French chest tube was then inserted and placed to suction... the patient tolerated the procedure very well.

"Hold still," someone says.

My spine feels as though it is being ripped into pieces. Once again, I had been rolled onto my side.

Medical Records 12/17/03: Yesterday pain service was consulted and epidural was placed... She did sleep last night.

One of the mothers from the violin recital is at my bedside. I don't know her very well. "I thought you might like this CD, and I brought you books." She's bobbing her head and clenching her hands together as though she's flustered.

I ask her what day it is. "Tuesday," she replies. "I've got to get out of here. I've got to take care of Elizabeth, go to work, feed my animals," I say. "I'm sorry, but I have nothing to listen to a CD with. And my glasses are gone."

Friends come. People from our community drop in. Parents who have children in Raymond's and Elizabeth's grades visit. Flowers arrive.

People whom I don't know show up. Others whom I haven't met arrive and introduce themselves. I recognize their names from the community, and I wonder why would they want to be here? Their presence is disconcerting to me. I have no words for them.

Gradually, pain that is greater than being in hell (I surmise) usurps the shock. My head feels like a huge open cancerous wound on the left side. I reach up to touch it and bring dried blood and bits of glass back with my fingers. This light touch causes intense throbbing.

Medical Records 12/18/03:... Small area of increased density seen just posterior to the right frontal sinus on image... cannot exclude tiny subarachnoid hemorrhage in this location...

Three years later the hemorrhage mentioned in the medical records is not a memory to me. However, the side of my head still retains tenderness. There is no mention in the medical records of this lasting symptom.

The nurses stand over me to ensure that I order my meals. When the food arrives, seeing it makes me nauseous. They tell me they'll fix me a chocolate shake whenever I want one, and that carbs help the healing process. I can even drink ten a day if I want. But I don't want even one. I just want Jon to come, so I can tell him that Raymond died.

Jon comes when I'm sleeping. He rubs his thumb on the space between my eyes. I awake feeling him there. It is then that I truly know that he, too, has died.

On Thursday, the side table is shoved up against the rails of the bed. I sleep with the back of the bed cranked up and pillows under my back and neck. I reach over and find a tin with candied ginger and a magazine, *Bark*, that Sharon, a friend from my writing group, brought. A nurse opens the tin and holds it in front of me. I put one in my mouth. The little piece of sugared warmth begins to dissolve inside my mouth, decreasing the sensation of oral cactus.

Mike and Ruth arrive with Jon's sister, Judy, who has come from Arizona. They have visited other days, but I don't remember exactly when. This is also the day that my niece, Molly, and my sister, Mary, come and bring Elizabeth. This is the first day that I feel lucid. I will be able to retain some memory of this day.

Friday arrives, and so do a flurry of visitors. Among them are, Becky and Alan, Tawni, Jim and Rosalie, Jan, Judy, Father Ed, Molly, Mary, Elizabeth, Mike and Ruth (who bring my eyeglasses that Mike retrieved from the wrecked van), and Scott. Scott, our local funeral director, informs me that I need to start planning the double funeral.

Scott asks if I want a wake, or if Jon and Raymond's remains should be cremated.

What would Jon want? Raymond? I'm at a loss for what to do.

Alan, who is Jon's good friend, speaks up, "Jon would want to be cremated. We talked about it once when we were photographing."

"Raymond wouldn't want to use up the earth," I say, recalling conversations about death that Raymond had periodically sparked.

"Do *you* want to see them before they are cremated?" Scott asks.

I begin to answer and look at Elizabeth. "What do you think, sweetie?"

"No." Her answer is flat.

"No," I say, "I want to remember them the way they were."

Will I regret this? I wonder.

Pain acts as an unabated coupling of mind and body. My emotions remain detached until one night when the need arises to shift position. This should be a simple operation of pressing a button to raise the back of the bed. Any type of movement proves painful and difficult. In reaching for the bed control, instead of grasping it, I knock it down into the space between the mattress and the railing. As I pursue it, a fiery pain causes my muscles to lock up, leaving me in a twisted position. Attempting to straighten out provokes a panic, a fear of damaging organs, re-breaking ribs or vertebrae. I feel seized up. I can't yell for help, either; that would be too painful.

When the night nurse walks in, he finds me crying and gasping for air.

"Let me move you. Just let go, and I'll move one leg at a time." He does so, then does the same with my arms until I rest flat on my back. He massages my shoulders, the only part of me that doesn't hurt.

The same night, I become aware that my room overlooks the emergency helicopter landing, which lights up the rooftop of the adjoining building. Through my window I watch the rush of people scrambling to the helicopter's doors shortly after it lands. Blue, yellow, and red lights blink from the brakes and various mechanical devices, brightening the darkness of my room. As the propellers come to a standstill, the emergency crew lifts out a gurney and hurries away. The commotion subsides.

Jon was brought in on the emergency helicopter. He lived about two hours after arriving at the emergency room, someone informed me.

My thoughts race and I am left with no answers. *What happened? Did you know, Jon, that you were alive? Did you know what had happened to us? Did you know that you'd never see me or Elizabeth again? How did you feel? Could you feel? Was it your choice to go with Raymond? Are you and Raymond together? Was Raymond present to help you pass from this world? Were you in a room adjacent to mine? Could my bed have been rolled up beside yours? Could I have held your hand? Could I have talked to Raymond?*

———

The Salt River Canyon cuts deep into the Apache Mountains of Arizona. The descent into it, and the ascent out of the mountain on Highway 77/60 is winding, treacherous, and steep. I traveled this route many times in treks back and forth from Nogales to Santa Fe, or Nogales to Iowa, or Nogales to Show Low, Arizona, where I took my drama students for state competitions when I taught high school English and theatre in Arizona.

The last year that Jon's mom lived, we drove to Arizona with Elizabeth and Raymond, taking Sasha and Demetra, the dogs that we had then. When we left Tucson and began the tedious journey back to Iowa, we chose to go through Globe, Arizona, and subsequently through the Salt River Canyon. I wanted the kids to see it. Now that we lived in Iowa, chances that we'd pass that away again were slim.

A rest stop juts up at the bottom of the canyon immediately before the bridge for those who are heading north. Huge rocks guard the riverbank and are strewn throughout the flow where whitecaps send sprays of water in all directions. Near the banks, troughs form where boulders separate river waters, trapping some into calm pools. Small, smooth pebbles constitute the bed.

Steep and well-worn trails lead to and from the water. Elizabeth, who was six years old, and Raymond, only five, needed help. Holding Elizabeth's hand, we guided her. We held Raymond's hand tightly, too, restraining him from running full force into the deep water. Raymond's zest for experience left him without hesitations. He believed in acting before missing out.

Mid-afternoon in Arizona's August sun proved to be merciless. Maneuvering over and in-between perilous rocks to the ponds refreshed us. Not only were Jon and I holding kids, but we were also holding Demetra and Sasha on their leashes. They lapped up drinks and shook their coats, cooling us with the deluge. Raymond splashed and giggled. Elizabeth stood still, scooping up water, letting it escape between her fingers. I sat on a rock and soaked my feet.

Suddenly, I realized that the sun, now hidden beyond the tops of the ridges, had switched directions. Shadows formed. We had savored a whole afternoon in the deep reds and browns of the canyon.

On the way out, others in the river resembled specks on a microscopic slide. Far below us on the mountainside, lay a wrecked car. Rusted, it fit in with the color scheme. A slip of a tire over the side, it could happen so fast. Whoever rode in that car, did they live or die?

Slowly winding through the switchbacks, we climbed our way to the plateau.

At 5:00, the morning after observing the landing of the emergency helicopter from my hospital room, splashing water from the Salt River eases me from sleep.

This same day, the self-appointed funeral committee decides that a memorial service for family and close friends should be held in the hospital's chapel on December 23rd. After I've recovered, we'll plan one for the community who, in losing Jon, has lost its public librarian. Many knew Jon and Raymond personally and we will need to provide an outlet for the community's sorrow and shock.

The hospital's chaplaincy includes two Catholic priests, both of whom have visited me. The tall, overweight one attends our Friday meeting to plan the service. People file into my room. Family members, like Elizabeth, sit on my bed. Extra chairs are brought in, and some sit two to a straight-back chair.

When I inform the attending Chaplain of our plans, he responds testily. "Other patients aren't going to appreciate having two dead bodies paraded down the hallway." He doesn't know yet that the remains are to be cremated.

Another day a social worker sits beside my bed. I later would recall her as an ordinary-looking woman with an indifferent demeanor.

"Life won't be the same outside this hospital," she divulges, as though she alone is privy to this information.

I look at her and think of many things I could say, including, *Do you think I'm an idiot?* Instead, I ignore that statement. She offers nothing helpful to me.

Medical Records 12/22/03:... Patient has been seen by SW earlier in stay and is apparently uncertain of her needs at discharge... Patient however unsure if she can take care of her daughter at home and is struggling with asking for help. SW provided emotional support and encouraged pt to consider who she would be willing to ask for help...

I know what it's like to be the victim of metal and glass blown in by some tremendous force, to have family members' hearts burst from the impact. Due to the trauma, my memory sequence isn't chronological.

That ability decamped from my consciousness, leaving me instead with questions: How long before those of us left behind stop pounding the earth with heavy footsteps, and our souls no longer drag as dark impressions? Will we ever feel the shroud lifted from our tragic histories?

In a breath, Raymond passed on to another sphere. Perhaps this saved him from some sort of future torture on this earth. This I must believe in order to accept—if I ever can—his untimely death.

One action we undertake can severely affect those around us. For instance, I baked almond cookies for the recital, as all the families contributed to the receptions after the recitals, though I didn't remember them until we'd gone a mile or so. I insisted we go back for them.

You forgot the cookies. You threw off our timing, put us in the wrong place at the wrong time. Elizabeth screams months later, blaming me for the accident.

I didn't play the widow. I didn't wear black for any amount of time as portraying oneself as a victim doesn't erase tragedy from the memory. Nothing does. The feeling of desolation that remains after a brutal extraction of lives doesn't cure itself.

Each day, sometimes each hour, or even minute, I struggled with getting through with minimal emotional pain. Previous experiences with death taught me that with each minute, hour, day, and week, I'd gain a little leverage to detach my thoughts and create a new life, so crucial to have fresh and different scenes to draw upon. If all went well, I'd be building new memories. Though the intensity of pain never subsides, it can be stuffed down, managed by reinvigoration, allowed to surface only when it's voluntarily drawn upon.

Still, even now, memories randomly crop up, such as the fact that the truck driver was only twenty-five years old.

"He said he didn't see you in time," the Highway Trooper said when he came to my house to gather information for his report. "Maybe he was on the cell phone, or maybe he bent over to pick up something."

The semi hit our van on the left rear side, causing it to shoot forward and turn, leaving the left side vulnerable. The semi hit again, this time broadside. It took seconds. Raymond's section of the moveable seat didn't budge. The segment on Elizabeth's side jutted out when the back of the van was blown out, thrusting her forward into the back of my seat, wrapping her up like a cocoon, saving her from any physical injuries.

Jon and Raymond's death certificates report that the driver's blood test revealed a significant amount of marijuana, and that he was speeding. The driver of the semi was released pending the outcome of his tests. He ran from America. He has never been found.

Recently, I confided to a psychologist that I was a mess after the accident. She replied, "In ten years when you look back, you will realize what a mess you were after five years."

Sasha, my dog, died, too. Not that day, though. Not in the van, as I had feared in my mind's confusion in the hours after the accident, but eighteen months later.

Where Elizabeth and I live, there'd been no rain for two months. The topsoil is clay. Our veterinarian, Dr. Al—kind man that he is— buried Sasha, albeit in a shallow grave.

I had one dog besides Sasha at the time: Ella, a yearling. I fostered a crazed yellow Labrador and our neighbors had an ill-behaved Chesapeake Bay retriever who'd jump the fence and spend his days in our pastures.

One suffocating hot afternoon, eleven days after Sasha's burial, I napped, leaving the three dogs to their antics. Upon awakening, I looked out the window to the pasture. Something lay in a heap between the house and the pet cemetery. The two older dogs poked and pulled at it. Ella stood away, aloof, with ears erect. From where I stood, I couldn't distinguish what it might be, and it alarmed me.

The unmistakable putrid smell of death and decay permeated the outdoors. I ran to the dogs, yelling and screaming. In that moment, I felt passionate hatred. Hate with everything inside of me. Their violation of Sasha's remains unleashed a rage so deep I could have beaten those two accomplice dogs to death. The venom that boiled in my psyche shocked and frightened me. Never before had I felt anything so forcefully negative toward any other being.

I tried not to look at the corpse, the eye sockets, the dirt-coated fur falling from the skin with each movement. I rolled it onto the kids' sled, the only thing I could think of to transport the carcass and return it to the grave. Using bricks and cement blocks, I hoped to prevent subsequent digging.

Afterward, I no longer wondered if I'd needed to see Jon and Raymond's bodies before the cremation.

"Where's your valentine?" a college-age man working the counter at Bruegger's Bagels asks.

"I don't have one." I no longer ask myself if I should tell my story. I never have told it to strangers.

I'm wearing a Northwoods blue-wool coat.

"With that beautiful coat, you should have a valentine," he says.

I have learned to shift conversations to the other person. "Where's your valentine?" I ask him.

He and the other workers kid around about girlfriends and valentines, and I escape with my lunch to a table where I realize that this is what I do frequently: dodge conversations or questions that leave me numb, such as, *How many children do you have?*

One day, Elizabeth heard me say that she is my only child.

"What about Raymond, Mom?"

For many months, to mention Raymond's name threw me into uncontrollable sobs. Others are uncomfortable with grief, especially those who have never experienced it. On my good days, when I'm not tired, I can safely talk about Raymond without crying. On days when I cannot, I do not mention him unless it is to someone who knows me well. It's not that I want to forget Raymond, as Elizabeth discerned. Rather, it's that he is still so deeply a part of me that I cannot let him go, I cannot part with his jokes, his smile, his enthusiasm, his hugs. Describing these feelings to someone with no knowledge of tragedy, or of loss, is a challenge.

When the car that rolled, tumbled, twisted down the mountain side of the Salt River Canyon came to rest, relatives and friends of the passengers in that automobile passed along the news. What were those words? Did their lives turn into a private war as they battled the powers of desolation? Had those passengers once spent an afternoon of quiet bliss, allowing the waters of the river to flow over them?

That image of one small segment of my family's lives, the hours spent deep within the entity of the Arizona earth, appeared to me while in the hospital because it was one of the few times that, as a family, we shared complete contentment.

The Salt River Canyon is where I retreat, within, to cool the fires of destruction.

CHAPTER
Two

PLANTING SEEDS

S unflower
  (For Raymond)

Autumn's dry air
turning
Yellow floret brown
nothing
Bird pecks frozen empty
husk

Wind-fall fruit
Promise
Stalks rattle
tribute
broken
How long is Winter?

Cotyledon green
emergent
Yellow floret spreads
immense
Facing east
Anticipating
Sun's first ray

When I lived in the country in Iowa, I cultivated a garden. As the cool earth exposed spinach, beets, onions, green beans, tomatoes and other seedlings, volunteer sunflowers sprouted amongst the rows. These sprouts would have been delicious in a salad or sandwich, but I could not weed them out.

By August, after weeks of intensely hot days, six inches or more in diameter with heights of eight to ten feet, supported yellow and orange flowers heavy with seeds. Huge leaves hung, shading other garden plants. At maturity, these monumental flowers stood as stead-fast reminders of Raymond, my son, whose death I have continued to grapple with.

I met Raymond and his sister, Elizabeth, shortly before Raymond's fourth birthday. With the children's social worker, my husband, Jon, and I visited their foster home. Their sun had been "obliterated" in early childhood by abuse and neglect. But Ray, an optimistic little boy, overpowered his oppression and overcame the scars on his "battered crown," words Allen Ginsberg used in his poem, "Sunflower Sutra" (1955). Thoughts for the poem originated as Ginsberg and Jack Kerouac sat by a railroad, surrounded by human detritus. Until that day, Ginsberg didn't know the sunflower.

...corolla of bleary spikes pushed down and broken like a battered crown, seeds fallen out of its face, soon-to-be toothless mouth of sunny air, sunrays obliterated on its hairy head like a dried wire spider web...

As he observed the helianthus, his perception of it changed, causing a revelation. He then compared human nature to it, seemingly out of place in the crude industrial landscape, though of "perfect beauty":

We're not our skin on grime, we're not our dread bleak dusty imageless locomotive, we're all beautiful golden sunflowers inside, we're blessed by our own seed and golden hairy naked accomplishment-bodies...

I had kept a garden at our home in town where Ray became fascinated with growing plants, especially flowers of the borage family that noticeably rotated, placing their blooms in direct sunlight. Ray favored the sunflower and planted its seeds wherever he pleased. As a little boy, if seedlings got mowed over, or stepped on, he'd cry, tears gushing down his cheeks.

We moved to the country after Elizabeth turned ten and Ray nine. At our rural home, he learned to start seeds in protected places, as with the bunch he meticulously placed to express brotherly love for Elizabeth. The summer before he died, at eleven years old, he carried limestone rocks from the remains of a schoolhouse foundation on our property. Several feet from Elizabeth's bedroom, on the north side of the house, he stacked the stones to about ten inches high, forming a small circle. In the center, he planted seeds. By summer's end, Elizabeth could stand at her window and see, at eye-level, the gigantic bloom of a perfect yellow sunflower.

During that time, in reading Ginsberg's poem, "Sunflower Sutra," it struck me Raymond bore resemblance to a sunflower, and that he had been properly named. *Raymond* means *light of the world*. As dusk approaches, the sunflower's petals fold, its big head hangs. At dawn the head raises, worshipping the sun like a proud person throwing back his shoulders, boasting color and character. Raymond had a deep sensitivity. He folded in when hearing of human and animal oppression. He rebounded by opening up: joking, expressing himself through music and drawings, laughing, and by doing something nice for someone else.

After dinners, before I rose from my chair to wash dishes, Ray, as an older child, would stand behind the oak straight-back chair where I sat.

"Mom, this is what I'll do for you."

His strong thumbs pressed into the softness of my shoulder. I rested my fork on my plate. The tension that had built up from a usual day of running the children to all the places they needed to be, supervising piano and violin practice, working my job, and cooking supper, released by such a small gesture of appreciation.

Life with Ray, though, had not always been so easy. Early in my life, I realized many children need homes, which led me to reject wanting biological children. I also have nine nieces and nephews, all born within seven years of each other. The first one came in my eleventh year. In essence, we grew up together, and I babysat, periodically caring for them for extended periods. By the time I reached my late teens, experiences with babies and young children had sated me.

Jon and I married in our mid-thirties. It was a first marriage for both of us. I convinced him to join me in taking preparatory classes to become adoptive parents. Once certified, several months passed before a social worker from the Department of Human Services asked us to meet Elizabeth and Raymond. Our initial visit allowed the social worker to observe us interacting with the children, to note the children's response to us, and to see our reactions. The satisfactory outcome of that meeting led toward more visits, then outings, then overnights at our home.

When I first sat on the couch in their overwhelmingly cluttered foster home that reeked of cigarette smoke and had windows sealed in plastic, an overly thin little girl, Elizabeth, ventured to sit on my lap. Across from me, Raymond, with unkempt Afro hair seemingly with its own sprouts, hid behind a big stuffed chair. He occasionally peered out and gazed at us with expressive brown eyes. The social worker told me that Raymond had always been the outgoing one, that Elizabeth hung back, reluctant to participate in new situations with unfamiliar persons.

On that day, I wore a plaid-flannel dress and tights. Serendipitously, five-year-old Elizabeth also wore a plaid-flannel dress and tights. Drawn in by our similar taste in clothing, she felt comfortable with me. I assumed that because she let down her defense, Raymond chose vigilance to uphold their inherent bond.

On our first outings with the children, straightaway Ray demonstrated strong will. One day we took them to a city park playground. All went well for two hours until we decided to leave. Ray, not wanting to stop swinging, voiced his opinion. "I don't want to go and I'm not going to."

We both said, "No, we need to leave."

"No," Raymond said, "We leave when I say so." Then he jumped from the swing and ran. At first, I thought he would not go far but, in no time, he had made it to the bend of the large pond. I sent Jon after him while I held Elizabeth's hand. It took Jon a few minutes to catch up with Ray, who by then had stopped to inspect the flowers in the nearby botanical garden. When Jon did capture Ray, he tossed him over his back like a sack of sunflower seeds. Ray pumped his little legs up and down and beat his fists on Jon's back.

"You'll have to quiet down before I let you go," Jon said. Jon's approach to this episode pleased me, as I had doubted his know-how with young children. He had not spent time with the preschool ages.

On the next outing, to celebrate Ray's fourth birthday, we took Elizabeth and Ray to a restaurant where Ray asked for Jell-O and cottage cheese. After the waitress brought the dishes, Ray asked for salt and pepper. I held onto the saltshaker, intending to salt his food, but he grabbed the container from my hand and before I could snatch it back, he opened the top, which must have been loose, and dumped it all on his dish.

"Oh, look!" He yelled and tossed the food on the floor underneath the table.

Jon and Elizabeth, sitting on the other side, watched.

"Raymond. Not good," I said, aghast that a child would do such a thing, yet I managed to keep my composure. "Next move like that and you're out the door."

He immediately jumped up and, standing on his seat, looked over the booth at the customers around us and yelled, "All these people LOVE me! They won't let you do anything to me!" And then he sang, "You *Are* So Beautiful" in perfect tune, emphasizing the word "are."

Immediately, everyone at the tables around us began to clap and laugh.

I took Ray outside. Because of his young age, I believed he deserved another chance. Besides that, his musical ability had enchanted me. Until then, I hadn't heard him sing. We returned to the table, but he wouldn't eat. He just jabbered in an extremely loud voice.

"Okay, time to go," I said. On the way out, I detoured to the restroom with the children. As I helped them wash their hands, Ray prompted, "Let's do it, Sissy." Both began screaming over the noise of the hand dryers. Loud enough to trigger two waitresses to barge through the door. One said that she expected I might be spanking the children for their table behavior. The children interpreted the two women's appearances as an encore and the screams turned to blood-curdling yelps. I thanked the waitresses for their concern and gathered the children by their shoulders, hurriedly escorting them to the parking lot where Jon waited in the car.

When at home, without the children, I began to worry that I'd not be able to give them what they needed, persistence in discipline, redirection of inappropriate behaviors, love, patience, guidance to find the right niche, and most of all self-belief. Despite occasional assistance from Jon, I doubted he would help much. To date, the children had connected with him by sitting on his lap or inviting him to read. He had participated actively when Ray had run from us, but only with my instigation. When the children needed a word of discipline or of encouragement, Jon generally looked to me for follow-up. Camera in hand, he most often occupied himself with documenting us, freezing our actions in history. The children and I played games of chase and tag. They climbed onto slides. Raymond pushed himself to go down swiftly and Elizabeth grabbed the sides and held tightly. I would stand at the bottom to catch them.

When the children began their overnight visits, I alone did their laundry, gave them baths, and helped them dress. Jon watched from an easy chair while I did such chores as sort clothes, scrub the kitchen floor on hands and knees, and cook food the children would eat. Invariably, one of the two threw their food to Sasha, one of our two dogs who sat under the table.

"You cannot do that. If you don't want it, leave it on your plate," I said each time it happened. Both children continued testing us. Each one of their misbehaviors evaluated our worthiness as parents. Could they trust us? Would we keep them?

"Don't use that tone of voice with them," Jon said, all of us still at the table. "Your impatience shows."

I pursed my mouth and glared at him. My reactions should not have been discussed in the children's presence.

Alone with Jon, I suggested I might not want to adopt. The children had yet to move in with us. Jon adamantly insisted we had already made a commitment. Legally, we had not. Given that, I called the three social workers involved in the children's welfares and set up a meeting.

In our living room, with Jon there, I said, "I don't know if Jon's and my marriage will last. Knowing this, how do you feel about us adopting the children? I also don't know if I'll make a suitable mother."

Jon interjected, "Jacinta doesn't know her mind. She doesn't know *what* she wants but truly she wants these children."

His statement threw me off guard, as I suppose my saying that we might divorce had done to him. Consequently, the social workers listed reasons we should go forward with the adoption and I, feeling confused, agreed. The social workers addressed the possibility of divorce. One never knew what might happen in the future and if separation did come to pass, the children would deal with it as all people do when confronted with what life hands out. That made sense to me. I also worried what would become of the children if we didn't invite them into our family. On the other hand, I knew raising them would be a struggle because of their rough start in life. Jon undermining my influence while refusing to help bothered me, too. His interrupting and speaking for me to the social workers made me furious, though I stuffed that down inside, at least for the time being. The children's need to be taken out of their present situation, to be assured a "forever" home and be a part of a family, held priority over any would-be arguments.

I had three reasons to stick with the children, whether or not Jon helped. My father, an orphan, had died two months before we met

Elizabeth and Raymond. One of his last requests to me was "to open my heart to children, not just animals." I wanted to honor his wishes.

I also saw that the children had a tight bond. During one of Jon's and my visits to the foster home, Elizabeth and Raymond disappeared to the kitchen while the adults talked. Elizabeth helped Ray climb onto the counter to get snacks out of the cupboard.

"You get out of there. You're not to be climbing on the drawers," the foster mother yelled, waving a wooden spoon in the air.

"You aren't supposed to yell at us," little Ray said.

"You can't spank us," Elizabeth said.

They stuck up for each other. I liked that.

I heard my father's agitated voice, "When you and Mark were kids, nobody could correct one without the other getting in on it. You were like glue, always protecting each other."

Though four years apart, my brother, Mark, and I understood each other in a way no one else did. We accepted each other. We loved and trusted the other simply and without judgment. I saw this rapport in Elizabeth and Raymond. The professionals in their lives had concerns that neither child would be able to make attachments due to their mistrust of authority. I suspected they would eventually overcome that skepticism, as no child who cared for a sibling in the way they did could be thick-skinned.

Something else weighed on my mind. As a college senior, I had done coursework at a mental health institute where I had become a Big Sister to a ten-year-old girl, Dawn, who lived in a broken household. Her mother had had several children by different men, some of whom abused her and her siblings. Dawn told me her stories. I worked with her therapist, so I knew her truth. One time when I picked her up to take her to a movie, she got into my car, shielding her bruised and puffy face with her hand.

"It's my fault, Jacinta. I backtalked," she said flatly. After we talked, I hoped I had persuaded her to call the police immediately should something like that happen again. In my naïve world, I had no idea it might not be an option for her.

The next time I went to see her, a man answered the door and said she wasn't there. Over the course of that summer, I stopped in occasionally and whoever opened the door told me the same. Because I had graduated, I no longer had an affiliation with the institution. Attempts to stay in contact with her were my own. Eventually, I quit trying. Then, one day I received a letter from Dawn. She had been placed in the state mental institution for attempted suicide. I made the two-hour drive to see her but when I arrived, a staff member said I could not see her, nor should I contact her. A few weeks later, I tried again to no avail. Then I wrote her and never received a reply. I felt that I had let her down.

Though almost twenty years had passed since my friendship with Dawn, I still thought of her from time to time, wondering if she had felt abandoned by me and by others. I thought that adopting and caring for Elizabeth and Raymond might save them from a life like Dawn's.

The social worker moved Elizabeth and Raymond to our house on July 17th. From that day on, I considered them my children. I'm not sure how Jon thought of them. We didn't speak about our emotions. I no longer remember if he introduced them to others as his daughter and son.

As foster parents, we abided by a six-month probationary period before we could legally adopt them. Valentine's Day marked the six months. Riding the rickety elevator in the county courthouse, Elizabeth clung to my skirt. Her height reached to only an inch above my knee. Ray, even shorter, walked in circles until the bell rang, informing us we had arrived on the fifth floor. Immediately out, Ray ran and slid like an ice skater on the old green marble hallway. Jon said, "No," grabbed his hand and restrained him, although Ray tried to wrench free.

"Not a place to run, Ray. You could run into someone and hurt yourself and them," I said.

At the hall's end, our social worker's supervisor stood, raising his hand to beckon us. "This way," he addressed the children and opened the office door.

Four wooden armchairs sat in front of the judge's desk. "Please sit down," the judge said, after she shook each one of our hands.

I sat and Elizabeth climbed in my lap, still holding my skirt. Jon sat next to me, and Ray stood between our two chairs, one arm wrapped around Elizabeth.

"How do you find parenthood?" The judge looked at me.

"Exhausting," I said, "But after these last few months, I can't imagine life without Elizabeth and Raymond. Their presence has filled our extra bedrooms, and the whole house. Their behavior is fatiguing. They never stop testing us, but watching them learn and soak up new information is amazing. They also have an incredible bond with each other. Such love, and it's admirable how they stick together."

"Agreed," Jon said.

The judge then addressed Elizabeth and Ray. "Are you happy with your new parents?"

Ray said, "When I'm not in time out."

I held my breath, but the judge laughed. "And you, Elizabeth?"

Elizabeth nodded and scooted closer into my chest.

Ray said, "Do we have any other choices?"

Again, the judge laughed. Then, looking at the children, she explained that Jon and I would answer some questions and sign papers in front of her so that the two of them would have a "forever" home. I wondered if that meant anything at all to them as they had been in and out of foster homes.

"Jon and Jacinta, are you willing to be the parents of these children for the remainder of their lives?"

"Yes, we are," we answered. I wrapped one arm around Elizabeth and put my hand on Ray's shoulder.

"Are you prepared to provide for them financially and include them in your wills?"

"Yes, we are," we answered.

I watched the judge's soft face, the crow's marks around her eyes, the wrinkles that moved around her mouth as she spoke. I wondered if she had adopted children, but I couldn't think how to ask her in a way that wouldn't sound nosey. I looked at the law books shelved in the cases that surrounded her office and wondered if I'd ever have a life of meaning outside of taking care of these two children.

Then I thought about reading to Elizabeth and Raymond, how they squealed in delight at the stories and pictures in the children's illustrated books. They loved learning facts about animals, the sky, just everything. How learning to read at their late ages enthralled Ray and frightened Elizabeth, as she feared she would never be able to. How delighted they had been with their first new pair of shoes, two sizes larger than the ones they had been wearing purchased from Goodwill. These incidences, rewards, kept me going and got me past Ray's blood-curdling screams at bathing time, and their defiant refusals when asked to help with age-appropriate chores, like putting utensils on the table.

At forty-three years old, after catering to Jon's demands for seven years, I hoped to eventually pursue a career of my own. Yet, I had discovered in several months of living with Elizabeth and Raymond that mothering two special-needs children required full-time commitment. Realizing I had been handed a vocation, planned or not, I set my heart on teaching them the meaning of family, a crucial lesson that when learned I hoped would propel them toward a stable future.

In public school both children stood out because of their delayed learning and emotional disabilities. Many children ostracized Ray due to his skin color, as well. Caucasians constituted ninety-nine percent of the district's population, which eased Elizabeth's fitting in as she is white. Ray's natural affinity for people eventually brought him acceptance, though not before having to prove himself. Jon and I could both see that Ray was bright and gifted. Elizabeth, too, which sometimes became a problem; she would put Ray up to mischief. Trusting her, he would listen to her instructions but not to ours, nor to other adults'.

On Ray's sixth birthday, Jon and I gave him a short list of restaurants to choose from to go for dinner. He could also pick one schoolmate to accompany us. When we told him this a few days before the celebration, Elizabeth leaned over at the dinner table and whispered in his ear. Immediately, Ray gave us a response.

"Chuck E. Cheese," he said.

Elizabeth leaned toward him again and said something.

"I want to take Jim," Ray said.

"That doesn't sound like you, Ray. You hardly ever play with Jim at school," I said. "Elizabeth has a crush on him. Are you sure he's your choice?" I looked at Jon, who shrugged.

"No, I'll take Matthew," Ray said.

Immediately Elizabeth whispered to him. Ray then said, "No, I want to take Jim."

"Suit yourself, but remember it's your birthday and your choice," I reiterated.

Ray turned to Elizabeth and yelled, "It's my birthday, Elizabeth! I'll choose."

Then, he got up and left the table. In the end, he did invite Matthew, a boy on the autism spectrum. During Ray's younger years at school, he considered Matthew his best friend. And, even as Raymond made more friends, he stuck by Matthew. They had a comradeship, as both were different from the norm and spurned by other children. Ray spent most of his school recesses playing ball with Matthew. When other children picked on Matthew, Ray would tell them to go away, to let Matthew be. He reinforced his words by telling the tougher ones they'd have to fight him if they continued to harass his friend.

Many times over the years, Ray would come home from school agitated, or worse, in tears. Jon, still at the library, wouldn't be witness to these discussions.

"Mom, three guys hide in the bushes on the path to the bus. When I leave the building, they jump out and grab me, try to take my back-pack. Sometimes they hit me," Raymond explained. He stood by my office chair, nervously playing with a rock, rolling it between his fingers. Elizabeth, behind him, rattled off the names of the boys. They had just returned from school and I, still engrossed in my own work, tried to focus in on what they said. Scooting my chair away from my desk, I looked at both for a moment. The usual smooth skin of their foreheads wrinkled in concern.

I recognized the names, pictured the boys' parents, the broken homes, the cloistered world that confined them. I doubted those kids ever had a chance to travel, or had someone read to them, or had an adult play a game with them outside of school. I had limited conversations with their parents at the town's pizza restaurant, or at rare times when they appeared at school functions.

As Raymond stood before me, I took both him and Elizabeth and wrapped my arms around them. These same boys, when they were all five years old, forcefully took Raymond's pants off in after-school day care. No discipline had taken place then, despite my uproar. I suspected one of their parents had threatened the daycare director. Jon, though also incensed, would not support me in pursuing whatever justice might have been available for Raymond. As a result, I insisted on taking the children out of daycare and arranged my job so that I could be with them after school. These same boys had threatened Raymond on the playground several times. They taunted Raymond and Elizabeth about Raymond's skin color, their music talents, and so many things. I doubted I knew the whole story.

After the attack from the bushes incident, I talked to the principal and teachers, alerting them again of my children's worries. But mostly, I coached Raymond and Elizabeth how to deal with this if it happened again.

"You must immediately go to an adult whom you trust when these things happen." And then I named several teachers whom I knew would not stand for such behavior.

Still, I knew Raymond had a knack for feigning innocence, as he'd been known to toss out verbal incitements. I had been called to the principal's office many times for Elizabeth's behavior, and Raymond had a paper trail, too. He had been caught more than once instigating name-calling events as the children stood in line at school. He had thrown food in the cafeteria. In PE, Ray continued to play basketball, ignoring the teacher's command to put the equipment away. Another time, when a substitute taught his music class, Raymond had loudly told her she didn't know anything, and preceded to play the piano instead of giving the woman his attention and respect.

Despite his naughty behavior, when called upon for his lack of courtesy, he would offer a deeply felt, "I'm sorry." Knowing he'd hurt someone else's feelings brought about his sincerest apologies, and after doing so, his brown eyes opened like a sunflower.

Gradually, Raymond learned the art of negotiation, the importance of good manners and respect toward others. It did not come about in two or four years. However, isolated incidents that seemed insignificant accumulated. After school, Elizabeth and Raymond usually walked to the public library, a short jaunt to the other side of the football field where Jon worked as the director. I would come for the children after I finished with my job. Sometimes I would go home first, when we still lived in town, and walk our dogs to pick up the children. My dogs, as long as they behaved, accompanied me in the library. On a particular afternoon, as I stood visiting with another patron at the desk, Raymond walked with a classmate behind Sasha, our white husky.

"Look at his butthole," Raymond said in a loud voice and giggled.

"Raymond." I said, turning toward him, "You come outside with me right now."

"Why?" Raymond said in an innocent and yet challenging tone.

"Right now, or you will be sorry," I said and marched out, the dogs leading the way.

Ray followed, though nonchalantly. Obviously, he wanted to portray a tough persona in front of his friend.

Outside, I beckoned him to follow, and I took him around the building where no one could hear us.

"Who do you think you are?" I demanded. "At eight years old, you're playing a smart aleck. What you said in there was crude and inappropriate and you know it."

"What's it to you?" Raymond said, a tilt to his chin. I realized I had embarrassed him, which he needed given his behavior. But his tenuous relations with peers prompted him to behave outlandishly. He wanted others to notice him, hoped to gain acceptance in this way.

I exhaled and said, "Look, Ray, I've never been a mom before you and Elizabeth came along. Circumstances threw me into this job and I've no idea how to go about it." I paused. Searching for words to continue, I remembered Anne Lamott's writing that instructions hadn't come with her son. I used her idea.

"No instructions came with you two, Raymond. I do know that I love you and I'm trying my best to teach you how to get along in this world."

He looked up at me, his big brown eyes studying me. Then, he sighed. "I'm sorry, Mom. I'll try to do better."

Not long after that, the children's therapist and one of Raymond's teachers remarked that Raymond seemed more relaxed, not so anxious to draw inappropriate attention. I'm not saying he became a gentleman overnight. He had his moments, especially in the presence of an authority figure new to him. He also continued the struggle to gain acceptance from all of his classmates. But what I said planted a seed that began to grow.

One morning, as he practiced the piano, he stopped playing and banged his hands down, running his fingers the length of the keys. It sounded nice, even though it came as a protest. He had been playing piano for three years and had only a few months left of fifth grade. After the coming summer, he would be in middle school.

"What's up, Raymond?" I asked. Almost always, I sat with the children as they practiced music, helping them through places that needed more work on tempo or note reading.

"The kids at school are mean to me." His head hung over the keys.

"All of them aren't," I said.

"Well, no. But some are. Those same guys. They want to know why I'm black and live with a white family. They say that's not right."

"So, tell them that lots of families are like us. Tell them that they just don't know and that you feel sorry for them. But tell them nicely, Raymond. No matter what a person says to you, if you persist in being nice to them, joke with them when they say stupid things, you'll eventually win them over."

"Really?"

"Indeed."

Raymond lifted his head, put his hands to the piano keys and began to play. "I'll show them with music," he said, his voice in rhythm with the tune.

When Talent Day for the elementary school arrived in May, Raymond had perfected Bach's "Minuet in G Minor." Other students danced, mimed, played guitar, did acrobatics, gymnastics, baton twirling, and played piano.

When Raymond's turn came, he sat down on the piano bench. He didn't have his book. A minute went by. His hands stayed in his lap. Another minute passed. The crowd in the gymnasium grew uncomfortably quiet. Jon and I sitting side by side, glanced at the other with question marked looks. I began to fret that Raymond had forgotten his musical piece. But after someone coughed and the echo died down in the big room, Raymond put his fingers on the piano keys. He played beautifully, and simply perfectly. And then, without stopping he went right into it again. And again. Each time he played it faster and faster. I wanted to shout out, "Raymond, that's enough. Stop." Still, his fingers flew over the ivory and black keys, his feet tapped on the piano's pedals, and his body swayed with the rhythm. Finally, emphatically, he played the last note. A moment passed with no sound other than the reverberating piano chord.

Then, everyone began clapping and stomping their feet. I heard people saying things like "Yea, Raymond!" and "What a performance!"

Raymond stood, turned to his audience, and took a deep bow. When he came up, he looked at me and smiled his big joyful, playful grin. He sat down with his classmates.

After his piano recital, parents remarked for weeks to Jon and me about Raymond's talent and his tremendous performance.

Raymond seemed to possess innate powers. He had already proved himself in soccer in playing as a good goalie. His mixed media still life he created in art class had been chosen for an exhibition. Deep oranges and tints of red in sunflower petals reach out toward the sun, exemplifying the same energy. These shades, different from the ordinary prolific crops, radiate freshness. Diversity. They open like a meticulously composed song and then display themselves dynamically.

In middle school, Raymond joined the school band, adding the trombone to his handwritten "Wants to Accomplish" list. One afternoon, shortly after commencing the new school year, Raymond ran into the house from the school bus. He still moved swiftly as he had when small and compact but now lanky arms and legs gave him faster access. "Guess what, Mom! Those guys that give me such a hard time stood in line in front of me today. I had my trombone in my hands. They said, 'Hey Ray, 'spose you think you can play that thing?'"

"What'd you say?" I said, immediately concerned these kids might taunt him about what he loved most.

"I said, 'You darn tootin' I'll be playing this thing,' and I giggled." Raymond looked at me, his big brown eyes shining with mischief.

"So?"

"So, they laughed. And it wasn't a sarcastic laugh. We all started laughing and they said, 'Hey Ray, you're all right.'"

I took a moment to look at my son, to really see him. Somehow over the summer he'd lost the boyish look. His jaw had begun to fill out and sinew had begun to replace the baby fat. Raymond, my green seedling, had burst forth into a sturdy fibrous stem. He had survived harsh nights and cloudless days.

"I'm really proud of you, Ray," I said and moved to hug him.

But he stepped away. "Wait, Mom. You can only hug me at home now."

I cocked my head questioningly.

"I don't want the guys to see you mushing me." He giggled and grabbed me tight saying, "This is my constrictor hug!"

I would not know Raymond as a full-grown man. He died that year, two weeks before Christmas.

After Raymond's death, I left his room be. Occasionally I opened the door and peered in. I would enter, sit on his bed, hold one of his stuffed toys and gaze at his many books, games, and trinkets. An incessant ache would grow deeper and larger, engulfing me inside and out until it had nowhere to go but out my eyes, convulsing like a geyser.

One time after Elizabeth and I had a fight, I could not find her. After searching inside the house and outside, I went to Raymond's room with the intent of summoning his energy to help me. There, in his closet, she sat on the floor, clutching one of Raymond's sweaters. She had pulled from the shelves and hangers all his belongings including his clothes, Boy Scout badges, toy trucks and cars from his earlier years, his music CDs, and surrounded herself in them. At first, when I discovered her, I began to speak but when she looked at me with mournful eyes, I merely said, "Oh, Sweetie." I then left, quietly closing the bedroom door behind me.

Three and one-half years after the accident, Elizabeth and I readied to clean out his room. By "readied" I mean that for a few weeks we talked about it. We planned for a specific day to go through Raymond's belongings, and to replace the furniture and decorations with Elizabeth's choices, creating a space for her to entertain friends when home on breaks. She had transferred to a boarding school. We hoped that a new place without a constant nagging of Raymond's absence might lessen her suffering.

Two dreamcatchers, a naked troll, a Beanie Baby tiger, and illuminated stars dangled from the ceiling light where Raymond had attached them. We left those to swing free. His books, stuffed animals, the origami collection he created, his Scouting treasures, writings, music, and artwork we boxed up for Elizabeth to keep. The furniture went to a single mom and her son, who was one of Raymond's friends. Raymond's clothes had been sent to the Gulf Coast after Hurricane Katrina. Raymond would have preferred those in need be given his stuff.

Amongst his belongings, Elizabeth found a card I'd written to Ray when he attended Boy Scout Camp, the summer before he died.

> Already we miss you and you've only been gone for a day! ...I'm sitting on the front porch with Sasha and Jack. We are watching the goldfinches play on your sunflowers in the garden... We should make a garden plot next year that is strictly for you to plant sunflowers...
> I love you very much.
> Mom

A pair of fuzzy, leopard-spotted slippers rested amongst his things.

After Elizabeth and I returned home after the accident, she brought them to me one day. "Here, these are for you. Raymond bought them to give you for your Christmas present," she said. But grief stricken, I put them back in his room. I remembered when he made the purchase, though I hadn't known what it might be.

"Mom, I bought you a Christmas present today that you are going to love, and I would sure like to give them to you now," he said, grinning at me.

But I replied, "No, Ray, we still have more than two weeks 'til Christmas. They'll be an even better gift if I wait."

Raymond's smiled faded. "Mom, you always have to do everything conventionally."

Conventionally, a new word on his vocabulary list that he used frequently. When Elizabeth handed me the slippers, my throat clamped up and tears flowed. I regretted my rigidity. Now, the slippers stay in my pajama drawer, a reminder of his spirit.

After we finished with Raymond's room, Elizabeth returned to boarding school and autumn approached. The days became all too silent. Children's voices no longer carried from the woods below the house. The dogs no longer barked with excitement of playing with the children. The horses' whinnies became faint reminiscences.

Had Raymond lived, he would have been fifteen when Elizabeth and I sorted through his belongings. We would have listened to him play piano, trombone, guitar, and watched him play basketball, baseball, and run for the track team. He would have eagerly taken care of the animals, and would have been involved in Scouts and 4-H. He would have connected in all possible ways, engaging Elizabeth, too. Together, they would have continued to bike, ride horses, cross-country ski, and ice-skate with friends. My ears would fill in delight, listening to their duets on piano and violin. Raymond would have enticed Elizabeth to study geography, to learn names and locations of countries and rivers, challenged her smart mind with knowledge that, after his death, she resisted learning. Calm Ray had balanced Elizabeth's turbulence.

Raymond would have laughed and teased us, defied the shorter days of the oncoming dormant months, the dark months that drove us to moodiness, now swelled by Raymond's absence. Days after an early frost when sunflower stalks blacken in decay, petals droop, in the growing cold. Yet seeds in the flowers' centers remain, sustenance for wildlife.

At the sunflower's zenith, browns protrude and recede, displaying depths of variation in the pistil where the rays of yellow in the florets pale. Bright yellow dots the anther and the tips of the stamen. The ovule appears black, but in looking closer, a brighter color, a zest for light emerges from underneath the seedpod. As symbols of the sun, of energy, and of longevity, these heliotropes face and move with the sun throughout daylight hours, commanding shadows.

My Raymond, brown from his mix of African American and Caucasian heritage, could evolve from a pale complexion in the winter months to a deep caramel by summer's end. Raymond relished brightness and refused darkness. He influenced those around him, refused what he felt unjust. He had a way of looking into another's eyes with defiance yet acting kindly. Had Raymond lived a long life, I imagine him with an upward swing of crows' feet, revealing years of humor and accomplishment.

———

Seven years later, at the time of year when sunflower seedlings push healthy green leaves upward, when teenagers propel toward adulthood, Raymond's class graduated. I stood before them in the high school gymnasium. Their red and white gowns and caps stretched out before me, their nervous heads bobbing from laughing, happy to be on with their lives, sad to leave behind good friends.

These students had comprised a memorial to Raymond as part of the day's program. I had worked diligently to prepare a speech for them, an expression of my and Elizabeth's gratitude for their continuing to keep Raymond's memory alive. Elizabeth stood by my side.

Raymond used to ask about death, I told them. He used to ask about many things and like Raymond, we must continue to question what is right and what is wrong. Our life on this earth is only one in many. Some days will be rough, and when that happens, think about

Raymond. What did he do when life got him down? He played his music. He laughed. He looked to life's brightness. He had an indomitable spirit. Call on him for help. Some people are put here to help us learn and to help us see. Sometimes they come in different colors, and in shapes we haven't seen before.

Later that day, I visited Raymond's grave. A graduation balloon hovered over the gravestone. A note beside it read:

"Gone but not Forgotten. We all love you, Raymond. From, Matthew."

CHAPTER
Three

ILLUMINED

At dusk, I shut off the air conditioning and crank open windows. Here, a mile from the Cedar River, I hear barred owls call to each other, coyotes yip their conquests, and raccoons rustle in the trees.

The air is close, the moon shy of entire on this summer solstice. I go to bed early, exhausted from doing yard work during the strongest sun of the day. I'm alone with the animals, which I enjoy, while my thirteen-year-old daughter, Elizabeth, takes a weeklong school trip. Nineteen months have passed since my son, Raymond, and my husband, Jon, died. Five months after that, a truck hit and killed Jumpin' Jack Flash, one of my favorite dogs.

Lately, I've read about thin places. The Celts believe that areas exist within a natural landscape where a living being can join with the other side, with those who have gone before us. Celts thought that a person, in opening to the natural rhythms of body and soul, could communicate with another's spirit during the brightness of a full moon.

As I imagine what it might be like to meet my son now—he in another realm and me here—I detect that something's not right on this particular evening. I can't put my finger on what it might be. The two cats, Kimo and Maile, are active as usual, but their behavior implies a busy-ness that counts for more than play. Kimo, a black and white guy, jumps his nineteen pounds to the windowsill and meows in long drawls. His tail hangs, makes deliberate, jerky movements. Maile, a little brown and white female, swats and spats at Ella, my yearling dog, who paces back and forth. Maile lunges and Ella hurries to hide, trying to fit behind the toilet where her tail and rear end stick out. Timid Ella dislikes surprises, especially a scolding. Maile insists upon having order—her way. To me, everything seems out of whack.

Sasha, my husky pal and guardian of ten years, frequently moves in and out of his bed. Cushing's disease makes standing and lying down painful. He moves his legs slowly, double-checking his balance before he puts full weight on a limb. I run my thumb between his eyes, encase his forehead in the palm of my hand. I tell him, "It'll be all right." But tonight, this doesn't calm him.

I tell myself the unending heat and lack of rain makes us all restless. The last rain came in late April, about eight weeks ago, and since then the heat index continues to break records. Eastern Iowa needs periodic thunderstorms this time of year. We need booms to crack the sky, to release rains that stimulate soybean, corn, and alfalfa growth in the soils of our river valleys.

"Lie down!" I command. I take Kimo from the windowsill and plop him onto the bed, swoop Maile from the floor and put her next to Kimo. Immediately, they jump back to the floor and Ella pops up.

Giving up, I get into bed and pull the cotton sheet up to my chin. It cools me as it flutters down into position, creating a breeze. In the far distance, a dog barks. Sasha and Ella don't respond. But my horses, Max and Sassy, snort, and I hear them move through the long grasses not far from my bedroom.

These sounds of the night normally comfort me. Hearing wildlife takes me outside my world, closer to a life where boundaries and expectations have definition to those living within it, though intangible to me, a mere visitor. This visceral world touches a part of me that has no flesh. The part of me that just is.

Growing up in the country and having role models who appreciated both feral and domestic animals instilled this sense of security. My parents, farmers, believed their job to be stewards of the land and of its animals. Certainly, my early background formed my perspective that all have a right to life, and a right to inherent nature. Because I too have worked the soil, I respect these ideals. Cultivating fields and living amongst the earth's creatures developed my primeval philosophy. I believe that if I honor the earth then some almighty power takes care of me.

In moving to this property, I wanted to live in proximity to wildlife, to have space, to have some distance between my house and the next one. Instead of listening to neighbors' blaring radios and revved-up lawnmowers, I need to hear the sounds of tree branches swooshing, birds caroling, and frogs chanting beside the trickling brook. I must grow vegetables and fruits, tend flower gardens, clean stalls, make hay, feed the animals, tune into the sound of a John Deere B tractor putt-putting through the fields. I want what I call an authentic life, a simple existence, albeit my modern brick house labels me as something other than Arcadian. Nevertheless, my passion rests outside the limits of the dwelling: in the woods standing at the eastern perimeter of the property, in the rolling terrain and, in the way prairie grasses sway over its hills. I perceive a sheath of secrecy, a shroud, in this land, and it summons me.

Across the road to the west, Jon's and Raymond's shared grave-stone looms in the horizon of St. Joseph's Cemetery where Celtic designs embellish many of the monuments. Jon once joked that the burial ground provided quiet neighbors. Now he and Raymond partake in the silence.

Some nights I sit on the front porch retreating from the walloping heat. Through the haze of mirages, I feel Raymond's presence. I think of nights when he couldn't sleep and I rubbed his forehead lightly with my thumb in hopes of relaxing him.

Raymond's eyes closed. He said, "What kind of love is this? I feel you hovering over me, protecting me."

Now, his soul lingers. I feel his touch as I do Sasha's coat when he brushes by me, delicately painting an enigmatic stroke upon my skin's memory. On this night of unrest, I feel loving spirits, like Raymond and my dog, Jumpin' Jack Flash, envelop me.

Now, in bed, I doze.

About one a.m., I awake to Ella growling. She's at my bedside window. I jump up and peer out into the pale light. I see nothing. "No!" I say. She tucks in her tail, starts for her pad when Sasha yips, gets up on his arthritic legs.

More than tired now, I yell, "Look, I'm exhausted. Lay down!"

Sasha ignores me, stands by the window, his pointed ears turned up. Ella joins him with ears also pricked up. Four triangles in a row of focused alliance, a vigilant citadel. The shallow light entering through the window highlights their silhouettes.

They know something.

The cats march up and down the hallway, their tails frizzed. I go to the kitchen and, from that window, carefully scan the outside. Again, I see nothing. I hear nothing out of the ordinary.

"Settle down!" I command. This time they go to their places. I return to bed, fall into a light sleep.

In less than an hour, I awaken to a piercing scream from right outside the window. Loud and uncontrollable, it lasts long enough to terrorize us all. My frenzied heart jumps. A woman murdered? Sasha and Ella don't bark, they whine. Maile and Kimo cry in long, low-pitched wails, a way I've never heard before. The cats disappear.

I creep from room to room, from window to window, peering out. I focus on each object that looms in the eerie low moonlight. I inspect every shadow. Nothing. The horses seem undisturbed. The land lies still as if the bizarre hadn't happened. And then, I remember this: At the end of the day, as I called the dogs in, a strange animal stood on the cemetery side of the road. Preoccupied with chores and other thoughts, I didn't think to look closer. In the back of my mind I thought coyote, and let it go.

I didn't stop to look, to see if it had a white coat. Now, in the weirdness of these wee morning hours, I consider Jack, my dog who had a white coat with an underlying brown spot, ghostly in appearance, that lay across his back.

Before Jack came to live at our house, he had dwelled at a neighbor's who kept him chained most hours of each day. Whenever Jack could manage an escape, he would come to visit, forty pounds of white fluff hopping and skipping down the road to play with our dogs. At first, he wouldn't have much to do with the people in our house. When we tried to pet him, he'd back away and run, only to stop and peer at us from a safe distance. Gradually, though, he began to follow me around—I kept dried liver cubes in my pocket.

At times, Jack stayed overnight at our place. Eventually, Raymond and I convinced the neighbor that Jack had made his choice. With the dogs outside, we kept the lane gate closed. But Jack had a knack for finding the weak spots where he could wiggle through and the low spots where he could leap over. After two trips to the vet to have stitches where he'd gotten hung up on barbed wire, he conceded to the eight acres as home. Or so I thought.

With Jack, we had no need for a fence around the garden. He kept the rabbits on the run. He'd bring his catch to me and proudly display it, dropping it at his feet before gulping it whole. I never witnessed a dog eat so much in that manner, especially one as small as Jack.

One day, while Elizabeth practiced her violin on the front porch, Jack brought his prizes into view. Elizabeth came running into the house yelling, "Jack has four rabbits, and he's eating them whole! It's disgusting!"

I ran out in time to witness him swallowing one. The remaining three were young adult-sized rabbits, recently killed. In fear of what the bones and fur could do to his digestive system, I tried to confiscate them. But Jack wasn't willing to share, so he gulped all the faster.

Jack had lived with us about two years when Jon and Raymond died. Elizabeth and I couldn't return home for several weeks after the accident. My body, beaten and broken, allowed me limited mobility and no independence. During that time, friends took care of the animals. Dr. Al, our veterinarian, boarded Sasha at his clinic. Jack, appointed guard dog by caring friends, stayed home.

The night Elizabeth and I returned, Jack ran to me and gently buried his head between my knees. Wrapping my arms around him, I soaked him with tears, which was the first time I could let out my sadness. I couldn't sit, kneel, or lie down without intense pain. I slept a lot. Sasha's weakened legs no longer allowed him to jump up onto the bed. So, Jack stayed by my side. At night, he slept close, his body pressed gently to my arm. When I opened the door for Jack to go outside, he didn't stay long and waited at the door to be let back in. This continued until I began to strengthen. Jack gradually began to let go. He stayed out longer, went farther from the house, slept farther away from me at night.

One day, I found him waiting on the roadside near the gate. "Jack! You know better!" I said, "You have to stay home!" Jack wagged his tail a little and then, tucking it between his legs, followed me to the house. Still, I couldn't muster up the energy to look for the weak spot in the fence.

One morning at 5:00, when Sasha needed to go out, Jack whined and danced, barked to go, too. I let them both out, waited for Sasha to return and went back to sleep. Two hours later, my neighbor, Margaret, knocked on the door. Her son had hit Jack with his pickup truck. At first, I didn't believe her. I thought it had to be someone else's dog. Slowly, however, it came to me that Jack had liked to race that old truck. Margaret walked a good half-mile down the road and carried his body home. She waited while I hugged him, and gently stroked him, and cried. Later, after Elizabeth went to school, friends buried him in our family pet cemetery alongside Demetra, who had been Sasha's companion.

Meanwhile, Sasha's illness progressed. Cushing's Disease eats away at internal organs, and the chemotherapy used to help monitor the condition inevitably deteriorates the bones. During the summer's intense heat, I'd call him, but he would not answer. I would look for him and find him sprawled out on the cool paths of the woods. I talked to him, insisted he stand up and return to the house to sleep in cool air. Our return might take twenty minutes, maybe more, to traverse an acre of land. He would walk a bit, then stop. He looked at me with his big hazel, husky eyes. Then, he tried to walk a little more.

Now, less than an hour after the heinous scream, Sasha needs to go out. He paces up and down the hallway, his nails clicking on the tile floor. Usually, he needs to go at least twice during the nights. In my sleep, I listen for him. I drag myself out of bed. Normally, I wait by the door while he goes out and returns on his own. Not this time. I go with him. I stay by him. My pajamas cling to me in the heavy stillness.

Motion catches my eye. An animal, about Sasha's size, runs along the fence line toward the horse barn. Its tail up and long, like a dog's. Its coat illuminates in the surrealistic light. Sasha sees it. His ears perk up and momentarily his feet spread out. He arches his back and wags his tail, like a puppy who has recognized someone. One moment the figure moves lithely, gracefully. The next, no sign of it. Not anywhere. My eyes chase where it came from, then where it might have gone. Nothing there.

I herd Sasha back into the house. Reports in the news lately recount mountain lion sightings near Solon, in Iowa City, and along the banks of the Cedar River. I'm concerned for the horses. But wait. I don't hear them. No sounds of restlessness come from them. No running, bucking, nor snorting, all indicators of panic.

Inside, Ella snuggles in her bed. Kimo and Maile lay entwined amongst my bed covers, their usual nighttime place. Sasha lies down, too. For the third time, I put the sheet up, this time over my head. Many moments elapse before my heart stops pounding and allows me to sleep.

At sunrise, Sasha's nails click up and down the hallway tiles again. Reluctant to leave this prone position, I force my eyes to look at daylight and make my way to the door. Sasha and Ella go out. I check on the horses, they graze peacefully. No sign of a frightening night for them. The sun climbs, and with it, the heat. I quickly round up the dogs. As I let the dogs back in, the cats attempt to escape, but I block them with my foot. Until I know no danger lurks, I want them in the house. Once again, Sasha, Ella, and I sack out. Ella sprawls over my bed.

By 9:00 a.m., I'm on the phone. Frustrated, I call the Department of

Natural Resources (DNR) in Cedar County. A voice message says no one mans this office; call Johnson County. I do. I get another voice message: Out of the office. I don't wait to find out until when. I call Information to find other DNR numbers. Finally, I reach someone in Linn County. He tells me he doesn't know about mountain lions but takes my number and says he'll pass the information on to a DNR person in northern Iowa. I hang up. My eyes burn, feel heavy as river-bottom silt.

I lie down on the floor with Sasha and, before I finish getting comfortable, I'm asleep. In my dreams, Jack runs along the fence line toward the barn.

The phone rings. Slowly I pull myself up and answer it. I talk to Barney from the DNR about mountain lions, or pumas. He says many people report sightings, but few are valid.

"Did you check for tracks?" He asks.

I hadn't thought to do that.

"What did it look like?" He asks.

I say, "Maybe fifty pounds or so, dog-size. Kind of whitish, at least it seemed so in the light of the wee hours."

"A puma can be 120 pounds. Like a big, big dog," he says. "His tracks will be two to three times the size of a coyote, and, of course, they'll be cat-like." He chuckles at his own joke.

I tell him about the scream.

"That's exactly what a bobcat sounds like. No, Ma'am, I'm not coming to your house to shoot a mountain lion."

I draw in my breath. "Shoot it?" I question incredulously. "You'd shoot it?"

"That's what most people want me to do when they think they've seen one."

Concern for the big cat grips me. "No. No, I'd want to know how to keep my animals and myself safe. I wouldn't want it shot."

I picture a rifle raised; a big cat downed. Magnificent, solitary and aloof, muscle and stamina wasted. Wild knowledge lost.

I lament loss of control in those who believe the big cat will kill them. I fear not the cat itself, but for her. My compassion helps me realize grieving an absent loved one goes beyond the vacancy splayed open by such a wound. Impermanence of loss, something all beings must surrender to a higher power's irrevocable decision. Accepting mortal authority as illusory rescinds fear, for we find that eternal death lasts only as we know it in this life.

"You're rare, that's for sure." I hear relief in his voice. "A bobcat weighs probably twenty-five pounds, maybe thirty. It's that screeching that makes me sure of it. A bobcat's screams sound like a woman being murdered. And a bobcat wouldn't bother your animals. Probably wouldn't even scare them."

I've seen bobcats, but I'm too tired to tell him so. We hang up and I sleep for another hour, then I go outside. I walk along the fence and pay attention to spots where nothing grows. The clay has turned to cracked stone, impossible to find tracks. Even the horses don't leave a hoof print.

After filling the horse tank with fresh water, I see a dead rabbit. Adolescent-sized and stiff, though he hasn't begun to stink yet, even in the heat. If he had been there earlier, the dogs would have gone for him. Puzzled, I carry him by a leg to the fence and toss him over, so Ella won't nab him. His balled tail puffs where he lands. Looking at it reminds me I forgot to tell the DNR man that what I saw had a long tail. Bobcats' tails are only six or seven inches long.

I bring books home from the library. In the afternoon after the equinox, I lift Sasha onto my bed. He naps and I read while we snuggle. I search for answers to the horrific screeching, and to the ghost that disappeared before my eyes. Mountain lions do scream in the manner I heard but I have no evidence that such a big cat trekked on my land. I doubt that a bobcat prowled.

I suspect that Jack paid us a visit during the night. Mythology and folklore across the cultures tell of dogs being conductors of souls, transporting people between the realms. In one book, I stumble upon the definition of a banshee, or an Irish she-ghost, the death messenger: *whose appearance and weird cries are feared as the sign that death is near…*

And, in another book: *whose cries pierce the night like a terrorized woman...*

Banshees are she-faeries that come as personal or family guardians in tight situations.

I have found my answer. I stroke Sasha's ears. Head resting between paws, his eyes remain half-closed. "Jack is your guide, Mister Man," I tell him.

Ten days after the solstice, Sasha falls. He can't get up. Dr. Al takes Sasha to his clinic. X-rays show holes in two of his cervical vertebrae. I sit in a room and hold him. My body shakes uncontrollably. Wails I cannot contain burst forth.

"We'll meet again sometime, Sash," I tell him, the words garbled in anticipation of another loss. During the night, I dream that Jack and Sasha run side by side through the long grasses, over the hills. Raymond and Jon and Demetra join them. I am waltzing, my feet bare, the dewed greenness cool and cleansing upon my legs. A veil, thin as light mist, separates me from all of them. Yet in dancing, I become one with them.

CHAPTER
Four

KEEPER OF THE SHOES

Three months after Jon and Raymond died, the man who delivered my newspaper paid me a visit. Sitting at my kitchen table with his wife, the man claimed to be clairvoyant.

"On Sunday mornings, Jon stands at your mailbox." The man said, his arms resting on the table, hands out toward me as though he wanted to hold mine.

But I didn't offer my hands to him. I folded my arms into my body.

"How can you know that?" I asked.

"I see him. I see him like the vision that told me my stepson would die three days before he did." The boy had been killed with three other teenagers on a gravel road late one night. The driver of their car hadn't stopped for a stop sign and an oncoming pickup had plowed into them.

"Jon wants me to tell you he's sorry. He wants me to give you this." The man handed me a small jewelry box. Inside, a silver keepsake lay inscribed with motivational words that I didn't bother to read.

I sobbed. I covered my face with my hands. My nose dripped. The man's wife got up to give me tissues.

"We've upset you," she said.

I said nothing. My tears ran amok because Jon's spirit didn't come to *me* after our accident. I sobbed out of guilt for wanting a divorce in the months preceding his death. I sniveled for not loving Jon. Yet, I did not admit this to the visitors.

After Jon's death, I wanted to make him notable. If people remembered him—if I remembered him—as significant, it would atone for me not appreciating him during his lifetime. I should have loved him. I told others, and myself, that I did, believing that couples who are married should love each other. People don't have storybook lives, but I wanted to believe that others did, and that mine should have been. I blamed myself for our bad marriage that now, unresolved, hung in the air and crowded my brain, still bruised from a concussion and other head injuries.

I met with my therapist to cope with the grief of losing Raymond and my guilt about Jon. I resolved to confess to her that I didn't love Jon, convinced that doing so would relieve me from the oppression of guilt. Instead, during my few sessions with her, I wept about my daughter's behavior, about Raymond's death, and about being left alone.

After the visit from the man who delivered my newspaper, I complained to my counselor.

"Jon hasn't appeared to me," I said.

The therapist told me, "My husband came to me after he died. He turned on our music system and it played *our* song."

Jon and I didn't have an our song. I could not bring myself to tell her we had no joy in our marriage. Instead, I described the visit from the clairvoyant.

"My newspaper man insists that Jon gave him the message to tell me he's sorry. Sorry for what?" I asked her. I hadn't thought to ask the man as I assumed Jon had apologized because of our tense relationship. I didn't think to question why Jon came to someone he didn't know.

A few days later, I conjured up an image of Jon. He stood in the laundry room wearing his stained turquoise jacket I had thrown away before he died. I envisioned Jon with hands stuffed into his pockets, as he often did due to his ill-at-ease manner. The face stared at me. The big body of my imagination blocked the doorway that led to the garage, entrapping me in the small room. I had once watched Jon pick up a sofa on his back and carry it out of the house without help. Once, he had pushed me across the hallway.

I wanted to say, "You creep. You killed Raymond. You murdered my son." Although Jon had never been an irresponsible driver, I had never been able to rely on him in other instances throughout our marriage. With that stuck in my craw, and because Jon drove that day of the accident, I blamed him even though we had no choice but to wait at the end of a line of stopped traffic on the Interstate. The semi had hit us from behind.

"Sorry for the tragedy of your life," I said to the conjured image. As soon as the words tumbled out of me, echoing in the high-ceilinged house, Jon's image disappeared, and I realized how shallow my statement was.

Back in the therapist's office, I told her Jon had finally appeared. A volcano of sadness erupted from me. My body shook, tears poured out. I didn't tell her that I *made up* the vision. I needed to believe that Jon's spirit came to see me.

My therapist thought my sorrow derived from missing Jon. No. I had despaired of our staying together, certain that we had ruined each other's lives as well as the children's.

I used up half of her box of Kleenex and I still couldn't spill out that I felt ashamed for having wanted out of the marriage despite feeling so alone within it.

———————

The accident happened on a Sunday. Sometime during the following few days, I felt a thumb pressed to my forehead, a touch of calming. Was Raymond's spirit reciprocating for nights when he couldn't sleep, and I had rubbed his forehead to settle him? Or was it Jon letting me know he'd left this world? My delirium prevented clarity as I realized I had been in a serious accident and that Jon and Raymond had died. Yet, I had no mental ability to accept those truths.

On Thursday, I began to emerge from the stupor caused by multiple head injuries, shock, and the intravenous medications pouring into my system. On that particular morning, the idea of death infused into my consciousness in the same manner the liquid drugs ran through my veins.

Raymond is dead. I would never see him again. Never hug him, talk to him, nor laugh with him. Never hear him play the piano, see him play with the animals, nor play soccer. He no longer existed. Gone. The truth of it exploded in my eyes, in my ears, my chest, my arms, my legs. The ache of no more Raymond burrowed deep into my spiritual cavity. No matter how hard I would try to seal that space, the ache would continue to throb with no relief.

On the other hand, realizing Jon had died brought immediate reprieve. I felt lighter. Felt that without him, I could begin to live. And then, immediately I felt guilty. After all, he'd been my husband of fifteen years and now, having passed on, he had no way to defend himself against my allegations. Jon and I had strangled each other's creativity, damaged each other's spirits like a flooded river, swirling and angry, downs trees.

A daily self-query began: Why had I married Jon, and why had I stayed with him for so long? If I had left him, as I had tried many times, we would have avoided that accident and Raymond would still be alive. At least, I tortured myself with this assumption while reiterating details of our lives together.

I met Jon when I moved to Nogales, Arizona, to teach high school English and drama. He taught media and ran lights and sound equipment for school plays. Lonely in my new environment and in culture shock after moving from the Midwest, I enjoyed his attention. At first, he slipped Far Side cartoons into my school mailbox, offering me a laugh in the mornings before classes. It helped to relieve my anxieties, soothed my stomach and curbed the nervousness that caused me to vomit bile before I faced my first class each morning. I dreaded I wouldn't be able to manage the classroom discipline and that I lacked knowledge in my field. Both were untrue.

Having been employed there for several years, Jon educated me on the inside workings of that system. He let me in on the personal lives of the administrators and particular teachers. He backed me when the principal called me into his office, which happened frequently since I spoke my mind about such issues as the importance of writing and the need for less than thirty students in an English class (some classes had more than forty). I didn't believe in giving passing grades to complement a student's self-esteem, which meant half of my students failed due to either low test scores, no homework turned in, or no class participation. The school district hadn't built a framework to teach students that self-esteem came from within, that accomplishments, such as turning in a completed paper, encourages a sense of pride.

I did not realize, however, that in sticking up for me, Jon also covertly attempted to manipulate me. Instinctually, I fought his authoritative attitude. In the beginning, our set-tos occurred frequently during drama practice.

"Luke, stand with your side facing the audience and give this statement punch. You are, after all, perturbed." I said during an after-school rehearsal.

"No. No!" Jon shouted from the technical booth. Suddenly, he appeared on stage, prominently placing his wide body between me to face Luke, saying, "Turn your head this way toward the dresser, step forward."

Luke looked at me, obviously confused.

I stepped in front of Jon and faced Luke. "I'm directing. Follow what I say and what you believe your character intends as we talked about."

I turned toward Jon. "Who was hired here to direct drama?" I said in a quiet voice. Then, louder, I said to him, "We need you at the lighting station."

"It's my job. It's my and the students' visions for how this plays out. You're here to help with back up. Not to direct," I said later, the first night that Jon had interrupted.

"From where I sat, it didn't look right," he said.

"Then come and tell me that quietly. Let me handle it." I said, looking directly into his eyes. We stood at the same height. His well-rounded belly kept his sweaters from reaching his waistline and he waddled when he walked. His outward appearance irritated me in the moment. And I told him so.

Ignoring my criticism, he said, "I've worked with the best drama directors. This is your first season."

"Exactly. Let me gain the trust of my actors." I walked to my car and got in, slammed the door.

This was not the only time, each night after rehearsals, Jon and I would stand outside arguing after the students had gone home.

Each day, he managed to get in the middle of my work with the students. So consistently he denounced my decisions that I became weary of fighting and let him have his say.

Jem, who played Snoopy, turned his back toward the audience at the end of his song. In each rehearsal, I demanded he face us before singing the last words. When Jem didn't face front stage, Jon would say, "Good, Jem."

A week before opening night, I gave up, said, "Okay, do what the man tells you."

Immediately, Jon told Jem he needed to face the audience on the song's last words. Okay, I thought, Jon just needs to feel in control. If that's what it took to stop the bickering, then I could give in. I failed to realize then, however, that Jon had a control problem and allowing him to step in set the precedent for our relationship.

We had gone out to eat a couple of times to discuss the technicalities of the stage sets and the lighting. During one of these dinners, he described his home in the country and his cats and dog. He invited me to visit. I missed living in the country, missed having animals, and I missed hiking, something I'd always enjoyed. Jon related that I'd have lots of pretty spots to investigate on walks since he lived at the base of the mountains. Because hiking on one's own in the desert can be dangerous, I figured since he knew the territory, he could go with me. I accepted.

Jon's house rested in a yet-to-be developed area of a Spanish Land

Grant near Rio Rico. From the front of the house, the San Cayetano Mountains loomed bluish gray in the distance. On the other side of the house, the Santa Rita Mountains shadowed purples in the afternoon sun. Mesquite trees and saguaros covered the landscape between. Patches of Rothrock grama grass blew in the breeze. When I arrived, a black cat jumped from the roof into Jon's arms where he stood below her. He kept a ladder at the side of the house for the cats to run up and escape to the roof should a coyote chase them. That the cat trusted him enough to take a long jump into his arms impressed me. I liked the idea of coming for visits to see his "family," especially in a place where I could see for miles without houses interrupting the views. Eventually, we would spend hours after school and on weekends hiking to and around the wild area surrounding Sonoita Creek, a stream that flowed gracefully amongst rocks and mesquite at the base of the mountains. Eventually, I began to regard him as a close friend. He talked of growing up in a small town in Arizona. His dad had come from a farming community in Colorado. My dad had farmed in Iowa. His mother had taught elementary school and my mother had taught, as well. Though our terrains differed—his arid, mountainous and hot, mine of extreme temperatures and humidity—we both had grown up in small communities and understood the rapport between people in towns and farming communities. We both cared about the welfare of the students in our classes.

Our walks, viewing cattle cooling in the creek on a sun-beaten afternoon, brought me memories of the farm where I grew up, an environment I had cherished. I began to confuse Jon's friendship and our analogous backgrounds with a romantic ideal that we shared the same likes, dislikes, and the same values.

Though Jon had enticed me by demonstrating positive regard for his cats, he could also repel me with his possessiveness. One morning in the teacher's lounge, I struck up a conversation with a new, single, male teacher who had come midyear. We had several interests in common. We both liked horses and he liked to travel and experience new things, as I did.

In mid-chat, Jon barged in, demanding that I go to the school office with him. I excused myself, and, trotting along to the administration building, asked what happened. He walked on, his pants legs swishing together, not acknowledging my query.

"Why do I need to come with you? Am I in trouble again?" I demanded as we walked through the door and stood before the main secretary's desk.

Still Jon didn't answer. Instead, he asked the secretary for his class lists.

"Why do I need to be here?" I demanded of him.

He turned to me and said, "You don't. You can go to your class."

After school, when I attempted to confront him for answers, he insisted we could talk better at his house. We left the school parking lot at the same time, and I took an indirect route, one of dirt roads. I needed time to cool down. His blue Mazda pickup sat in the driveway when I arrived. I found Jon in his living room already watching TV.

I flopped down on the sofa. "Explain, please, why I had to join you in the office today at school."

"You didn't," he said, letting out a big sigh from the easy chair where he sat.

I waited, but when he offered no more information, I stood and said, "I demand to know what that was all about! I felt controlled." I stomped my foot.

Jon looked sheepish. "I just couldn't stand having you talk to Mike and I needed to get you away from him."

"I'm not your girlfriend, Jon. And, even if I were, would it mean that I could not talk to another man? What about having male friends? Don't you have any female friends? You do. I know you do. What gives you the right to tell me who I can talk to and who not?"

"Well, I don't understand why, if you're dating someone, you'd want to be with someone else." He sat up straighter and stared at me.

"Look," I said, "I've got male friends everywhere. Some are my brothers' friends. Some are my own. Some I do stuff with, even though they have a girlfriend, or a wife. But that doesn't mean anything more than we're platonic friends. Period. And, I don't see this as *dating* you."

I picked up my purse and my books, gave Falstaff, the dog, a pat on his head and left.

The next time I saw Jon he confided his little sister had died at twenty years old. He'd been twenty-one. She had a stomach hernia and didn't want to bother anyone with her discomfort. He bowed his head and clenched his fist. For a moment, I thought he might cry but he didn't. Instead, he told me that I reminded him of her. She, too, had auburn hair and spoke her mind. Imagining how I'd feel if my brother, Mark, would die, I immediately pitied Jon.

But I never thought I'd live with him.

I resided in a newer apartment complex on the north edge of Nogales. I had little furniture and slept on my futon pad that laid on the floor. Four weeks after moving in, I awoke early. Turning on my back, I opened my eyes to the early morning sun and looked up. Tarantulas hung on the ceiling above me. They crawled on the sliding glass door. During breeding season, these arachnids invade all possible places that can reveal a mate. I had been told this, having seen them covering roads and sides of buildings, but that they'd come inside hadn't occurred to me. My aggravated stomach, already squeezing bile in the mornings at the thought of facing rooms full of students, constricted. I felt weak and I covered my head. Moving cautiously, I scampered to the closet, grabbed clothes, and while shaking them out, stepped quickly into the kitchen where I held a skirt, blouse, and underwear at arm's length and checked them for spiders. I examined the other rooms and found no spiders there. I dressed, grabbed my books, and went to school early.

At school, I asked relentless questions to students and to teachers about tarantulas, but no one advised me how to rid my house of them. No one seemed to know, or at least they didn't want to tell me. Perhaps they found this *gringa*'s predicament to be humorous. I dodged a teachers' meeting after school to shop for an exterminator and purchased a spray bottle of Raid, a chemical that I had thought I would never use.

Back in the apartment, the spiders still hung around. With the Raid can's trigger under my finger, I opened the bedroom door and charged in like an FBI agent who'd found her criminal. I sprayed the ceiling, walls, and corners inside and outside of the glass door. When I finished, not one tarantula existed inside. All had scuttled out through the cracks of the door and one window and other places that I did not even know about.

Well, I thought, *That shows them. I bet they won't be back.*

Then, I let go of my breath and inhaled again. Immediately, I began to cough. My lungs had filled up with Raid vapors. I opened the window, went for a walk, came back and the smell still hadn't dispersed. My head ached. I dragged my bedding out to the living room, but it wasn't far enough away from the fetor. I spent the night awake more than not, worrying that I'd taken several years from my own life by inhaling the toxic compound. Later, I discovered that tarantulas bite only if provoked and attacked. Most likely, a local person would have captured the spiders in a glass jar and removed them.

The next day, another teacher told me that she lived in a little cottage out in the country near Tumacácori. The owners had an apartment attached to their house that had been recently vacated. By the end of the following day, I had put my belongings in my blue Toyota Tercel and moved out.

The new place had well-worn kitchen table and chairs, couch, end tables, stuffed chairs, and carpeting. The couch pulled out to form a bed, but I preferred to sleep on my futon, which I unrolled in the middle of the studio room. I used my unzipped sleeping bag as a bedspread.

In late winter, I awakened one morning to small black bugs strewn over my bedding. I threw the covering off and sat up. The bugs also blanketed the carpet, the couch, the chairs. When I moved from Iowa, I had brought a 1930s Hoover vacuum that one of my aunts had given me. Shivering in disgust and crunching bugs in each footstep, I grabbed the Hoover and began to sweep, moving the machine back and forth with long-arm motions, imagining that the weird creatures in science-fiction movies now pursued me.

For several days, each morning and each afternoon I had to vacuum. With each day, fewer bugs appeared and then one afternoon after school, I came home to none. The landlord, who pooh-poohed my alarm, told me they were carpet beetles, a bug that laid its eggs in the carpets and in the openings under floor molding. Others verified what he said, but they also cautioned me that the bugs would eat my clothing.

Within a week after the last bug left, I returned from school one afternoon to find the owner's house had been robbed of shoes, kitchen utensils, and his varied collection of guns that had been locked up. My area had not been entered. I had nothing of value. Until then, I hadn't known that immediately on the other side of the wall where I slept, a cache of various firearms stood in a cabinet. I had known the landlord had guns and traps, having cringed at the sights of bobcat carcasses hung on his fences. That those arms had been stored a wall's thickness from my head, disturbed me as even creepier. After all, I could also be prey, accidental or not.

That forsaken Mexicans passed through this area on foot hadn't concerned me. I felt they had a right to do so in search of better lives. Now, however, I realized that desperados also traveled that territory, making it less than safe.

Beautiful views had motivated me to stay there. Christopher Reeve's grandmother's property adjoined the place, and I often watched her horses grazing in the pastures that faced the Santa Rita Mountains. I had taken long walks with the owner's dog, throwing sticks for him to retrieve, an activity that calmed me after a school day. After the robbery, though, the aura changed and I felt I should move to a more populated area, further from the bandit's trail, as Jon labeled it.

At this point, Jon offered me a room. The region where he lived, though sparsely inhabited, tended to be more secure, so I accepted. He helped me move my things and on that day of transition, we fought about his lack of cleanliness. The bathroom hadn't been scrubbed in a long time, perhaps a year?

I knew Jon's unkempt and dirty housekeeping would get to me, but I hadn't thought it would so soon. For instance, it occurred to me as I unpacked my things that he had ripped out the kitchen window screen so that the cats could bring in their prey. One cat hopped from the window to the kitchen table with a half-eaten mouse. I expressed my displeasure and an argument ensued. Amid yelling at each other, I walked toward the front door. Jon didn't follow me. I sat down in a chair for a moment to catch my breath. I prepared to tell him I could not live with him, and I did not want to see him anymore.

He came around the corner and kneeled in front of me. "I'm sorry. Please forgive me," he said. "You are a good teacher because you care. I need you in my life. Please stay."

If I'd had a few more minutes to think, I would have permanently detached myself, but his sentiment about my teaching caught me off-guard, as I constantly worried that I let my students down. Also, a long time had passed since a man had expressed affection for me. Interestingly, Jon did not say he loved me. In fact, he never said it, though he would write it in my birthday cards.

Meanwhile, my father, a widower in his eighties, still living on the Iowa family farm, persisted in expressing his worries that at thirty-some years old I still needed a partner. For years, I had listened to him tell me I would be lonely. In the same manner that Jon's criticisms had penetrated my subconscious, my father's words pervaded my thoughts in unguarded moments.

In retrospect, I had grown up with controlling male personalities. My father had been an alcoholic. He stopped drinking when my mother died, shortly after I turned twenty-two. One older brother had been psychologically abusive. He criticized my clothes, friends, and activities I chose to do. He sneered at mistakes I made. I adored him because he was my brother, but being young and innocent, I had no concept that his mean teasing destroyed my self-confidence. Nor did I realize that growing up under that brother's version of sibling love would lead me to constantly question whether or not my feelings were justified. Due to the influence of both my father's and brother's warped attitudes, I would sacrifice my own opinions and perceptions to agree with another's for fear of offending someone.

To boot, Catholic guilt from my upbringing plagued me. Breaking a consummate union would condemn me to hell according to the church. Jon's mother, a devout Brethren turned Methodist, tried to convince me during her weekly phone calls that Catholicism and Methodism shared the same governing rules.

Jon's mother also emphasized that Jon and his sister who died had been as close in spirit as in age. It'd been a task, she said, for Jon to make new friends after his sister's death. He should stay put in the "domicile" he had created for himself. I shouldn't rouse him to move somewhere else, especially not to the Midwest where the only color was green. He would become lonely for Arizona's hues.

One time, Jon's mother told me that in junior high school, Jon had refused to do homework or to prepare for school in any way. After discussing this with his teachers, she took him to a psychiatrist who told her, after spending time with Jon, that he could not be blamed for his behavior; his teachers and the school system caused his problems. Jon was *her* son, and unlike her other three children, he had special qualities and needed to be treated with great care and love.

I listened to these themes of Jon's mother every Saturday in her morning phone call, which Jon said we had to wait for. We could not go anywhere until his mother had checked in. Each time, she insisted Jon hand me the phone.

When I told Jon's mother that I was thinking of moving elsewhere, that I didn't think I would teach high school for my entire career, she brought that up every time we talked. According to her, I needed to stay in education. I don't remember what her reasons were. One time, in the middle of our discussion, she changed topics and said that Jon had other girlfriends in the past. I wasn't the only one, but she wanted me to know that I fit in best with the family.

Thus, I worried that friends and families, both Jon's and mine, would think of me as a harlot and as an opportunist if I left. Once moved in with Jon, I chose to concoct reasons, albeit odd ones, to believe our relationship worked. His mother's name, Elizabeth, known as Betty, and his father's name, Merlin, struck a chord. So similar to my parents, Elizabeth, known as Betty, and Merwin. This had to be a sign, I thought. The countertops in his parent's kitchen, which had the same pattern, a 1950s boomerang, as in the home where I grew up, also indicated a basis in my mind for our togetherness.

These *reasons* gave me something intellectually to grasp onto, even though I was old enough to know better. Logically, I should have been able to break off the relationship. I thought, however, I would learn to love Jon. I had heard stories of marriages where love didn't exist until later, growing out of a respect for each other.

But I found some things that Jon did abhorrently frightening. In the wee hours of one morning, Falstaff barked continuously. Jon got up, went outside and began beating the dog with a broom. After he squealed and whined from the first hit, I thought Jon would stop. But he didn't.

I then got up and went outside. My feelings shrank. Many years stripped away. I became the young girl who watched my father in a drunken oblivion beat a milk cow that wouldn't go into her stanchion with a strap. As I had done years ago, I initially froze. After a bit, I managed to say, "Jon. Stop. Leave him." I grabbed for the broom, and Jon drew it away from me. He did put it down and brought Falstaff inside.

On two different occasions, when we returned home from school, Falstaff lay at the doorstep with his muzzle full of porcupine quills. Jon immediately grabbed pliers and went to work helping his dog. But Jon refused to castrate Falstaff or build him a fence to keep him from straying. Eventually Falstaff disappeared.

One day, we walked around the property. In the back sat a shed with spaces of one to two inches between each siding board. I'd always assumed it'd been a tool shed and I opened the door but found nothing inside.

"What is this for?" I asked.

"My dad had canaries. I wanted them and he needed a place to move them to, so we built this for the birds and moved them here." Jon turned his back to me, facing the mountains.

"What happened to them?"

He didn't say anything.

"Jon?" I asked again.

"I got busy with school…" He stopped.

I thought he'd say that he'd found another home for them.

"I forgot about them. Forgot to feed and water them. One day, I came out here and they were all dead," he said turning to me, a tear in his eye.

Horrified, I thought of how on the farm of my youth, I would have been spanked if I'd let an animal go without food or water. Despite my father's alcoholic impatience when an animal didn't obey him, he felt strongly about the health of the creatures that depended upon us.

Then Jon said, "I can't forgive myself."

He said it in such a way that made me feel sorry for him. At least then, I did. I would begin to realize, after a few years of marriage, that he knew how to manipulate feelings, to make people excuse him.

Had my mother been alive, I would have sought her advice. She would have pointed out the missing synchronization between my feelings and my intellect. Mom didn't waste words, if consulted to apprise someone of her observations. Her perception never missed. She used to tell me, "You can't change a man. If you think you want to, then he's not for you." Her voice of experience, I'm sure, from living with my father's alcoholism.

My favorite brother, Mark, had that perceptive ability, too. Several years before I met Jon, Mark had been beaten up and left for dead in Chicago. He had Hepatitis B, although we wouldn't know that until closer to his death in 2000. His failing liver made him taciturn, albeit cranky. Now, fighting chronic fatigue, he retreated from involvement in my life, contrary to how we had once been with each other. No longer wanting to travel, he wouldn't come to Arizona to visit me.

Meanwhile, I encouraged Jon to take a job on a Northern Arizona reservation. I had spent too much time in the principal's office in Nogales and had had my fill of that school's politics. Reluctantly Jon accepted the reservation position, even though his mother insisted he should stay in Nogales. I told him I would leave, with or without him. He said he would come with me if I married him. If I wouldn't marry him, then he would not want to ever see me again. I interpreted his statement as a challenge. Impulsively and stupidly, I reacted without giving it guided thought. That summer, we married.

In Kingman, I substituted and at the end of the year, the district offered me a teaching job. Jon, however, couldn't control his eighth-grade class on the nearby reservation. His administration fired him.

I wanted to teach there or move somewhere entirely different. Jon, on the other hand, wanted to return to Tucson. I refused as I knew for me to survive, we would have to live far from his mother's grip. She phoned frequently and he counted on her to tell him what he should do. As a compromise, Jon consented to moving to Iowa, which was our only other choice in his mind, as it was one of the few places he had visited. My father offered to keep us until we found employment and our own place.

Once moved back to my old home, my brother, Mark, came to spend a few days. On Mark's good days, he behaved more like his old self and not so irritable. He stood in the living room, tapping his feet, and burst forth singing the lyrics to "You Can't Always Get What You Want." Jon had just related the difficulties of finding a job in the Midwest, specifically complaining about the persnickety-ness of Iowans. Mark had ways of making a point, sometimes mastering it with subtlety, other times with forthrightness and causticity. He made those who took him seriously nervous. Those who detected the playfulness in his approach loved his dear heart. Unfortunately, for my sake, Jon fell into the former category and he didn't find Mark's musical display humorous, though I had. That said buckets to me.

I had moved to Arizona with all my possessions that fit in my small car and when I returned to Iowa with Jon, we came in a twenty-four-foot truck stuffed full. We stored our things in the barn at my father's place.

"I've an idea," I said to Jon one sultry June morning. We sat in the yard swing my father had painted red with our backs to the sun filtering through the hackberry trees. Jon looked at his shoes that barely touched the grass, ankles bending back and forth. I walked my toes up and back to keep the swing moving. We both faced forward.

"I'll help you load a truck. You take your stuff back to Tucson. Your mom would love to have you there."

"What do you mean?" Jon asked, a scowl on his face.

"I mean move back there. I mean, let me go. We're not meant for each other."

We hadn't yet been married a year.

"No, I'll make it work. You married me. You brought me here. I'm not leaving."

I threw up my hands. "Can't you set me free, please? I really don't want to be married to you."

He stared at me and said, "No. If you want a divorce, you'll have to fight me for it."

Immediately, I recalled the stories he had spread about educators' personal lives in Nogales. Specifically, I recalled his dislike of a particular teacher. Jon said her husband divorced her because he found out after their marriage that she was a prostitute. The husband got her retirement fund. True or not, I would never know. Still, unease kicked in for the worry of what he might do to shut me up.

Each time when I threatened to leave, he would preface a long oration with, "It won't be easy," and then he would continue with, "I can't go on without you."

That he couldn't go on without me now that he lived far from his mother was probably true. His dependency suffocated me and yet, I felt responsible for having talked him into moving from Nogales.

In Iowa, we bought a neglected craftsman style cottage. It needed a new roof, plumbing, new bathroom fixtures, new electrical lines. The kitchen cabinets had been painted several times over grease and dirt and the paint peeled due to the hasty fix ups. The first-floor woodwork had blackened from the oil furnace that still occupied the basement. Upstairs, lead paint covered the moldings and trim.

I spent my nights after work and my weekends with a face mask on, stripping paint, washing walls, wallpapering and refinishing. I made the phone calls and worked with the plumber and the electrician. Jon, somewhat adept at woodworking, set his efforts to making new kitchen cabinets, which we designed to match the originals. I continued to renovate room by room, though eventually I hired someone else to finish the kitchen. Jon fizzled out.

I did the grocery shopping. As I unloaded the bags, Jon would let the dogs out the door as I, arms full, tried to come in. The dogs, happy to see me, would jump up, gather around me, and prevent me from moving. Jon never offered to help, nor did he restrain the dogs as I went in and out of the gate and the door, to the car and back. Losing my patience, I would ask for assistance, but he would tell me that I had a nasty tone of voice, not one conducive to encourage his support.

He would cook if I hadn't yet started supper. He did do the dishes occasionally. I cleaned the house, mowed the lawn, planted, weeded, and harvested the garden. After plowing the garden and planting seeds, I would draw him a map of what I planted where. Some seasons, he replanted, placing other seeds in the rows I had meticulously cultivated. I walked the dogs, cleaned the dog yard and the cat boxes, although, technically, the cats belonged to him. Even so, I fed them and made certain they had water.

Jon began studies for a Master's degree in library science; the education I considered, but had to give up as we had no financial means for simultaneous educations. By the time we had been married for five years, Jon had been fired from two jobs, both in media in public schools. Both times, disorganization and insubordination of his superiors were cited. Because of those dismissals, I discovered he had been fired twice before I knew him. I, too, had several jobs in my time of employment, but had left them for better work conditions. After I married Jon, I developed trouble understanding supervisor instructions and the quality of my efforts degenerated. So deeply encased in a mismatched marriage, I didn't see that my unhappiness and Jon's constant criticism had affected my abilities.

Jon followed up on what I had learned early on, to blame myself for everything that went wrong. Eventually, my thoughts involuntarily turned inward. Saying what I meant became difficult, and my apprehension increased. At night, when I was exhausted from doing the housework, yard work, and putting in my own hours as a secretary and editor, Jon demanded that I sit with him at the kitchen table. He broached the same subjects over and over. Leaning back in his chair, an arm slung over the backside, he'd accuse me. He would say I'd used an incorrect tone of voice during the day to address him. Another time it would be that I kept constantly busy working, or cleaning, or reading. I needed to go places, to do things. I could never sit and do nothing, he claimed. Each time, his complaints were trivial in my mind, a waste of time to agonize over my personality traits. On trial, I had to defend my views on several issues, such as his mother, whom I felt smothered him; my need to keep my life and environment orderly; my meticulousness and attention to completing tasks; the distance in our relationship; and my friendships with other men who were my friends long before I knew Jon.

He especially held an irritation about my concern for my favorite brother, Mark. Additional judgment included what he heard me say to someone else during the day in casual conversation, whatever light-heartedness it may have been, of being friendly with neighbors, and, of my appreciation of cooking whole foods. He had no desire to eat healthy foods, and often left donut or sweet roll packaging, from which he'd consumed many in one sitting, where I might find it. I believed in eating nutritiously, which was one more habit Jon despised.

Sometimes he'd hold a pencil in one hand, tapping it on the table, demanding I talk with him. Or he might lean forward, elbows on the table, hands folded, indicating I had problems that needed to be addressed. Obedient at first, I wanted to make our marriage work. After some months, and exhausted patience, I scooted back my chair and said, "This is enough. Pay attention to your own foibles and once you've addressed yourself, then you can nitpick me."

Instead of considering my point, Jon insisted I had not spoken with respect. As a result, the nightly encounters began with him saying something like, "You can't demand from me. You must ask me nicely, as my mother does, to get results."

I'd stand, or lean against the kitchen wall, ready to exit. "After the nonsense you've put me through, how can you expect me to be civil?" Still, I'd be drawn into an unlimited amount of time, maybe fifteen minutes, maybe an hour of futile arguments. In warm weather, with open windows, I feared neighbors could hear us, although not one ever mentioned it.

I had taken in a dog, Isis. After she had been with us for a time, she learned to read us, and before we could say a word to each other, she hugged my ankles, shaking uncontrollably.

After these bouts with Jon, I found it difficult to sleep. One night, after we had gone to bed, Isis began to bark. I got up and went to her, downstairs. I spanked her over and over until her cries made me recall how Jon had beaten Falstaff with the broom. I stopped then and vowed I would no longer get into the trap of Jon's trials. Mostly, I escaped the altercations, but occasionally I got caught up, usually because I expressed irritation that his promises of helping with cleaning or with the yard, for example, went unheeded. Sometimes I planned for us to go to dinner and a movie. At the last minute he might become cranky and say that we had never talked about going out, and then we wouldn't go. According to Jon, any complaints on my part had to be due to *my* troubles in that moment, or on that day. I had no right to be irritated. "Are you having a period?" He often asked, impatiently accusing me of causing the discord. Incensed, I would lash out, claiming him to be insensitive and obtuse, which would begin a new round of angry shouting.

Despite our troubles, I swayed Jon toward taking licensing classes to adopt children. I had dreamt since my own childhood of adopting. When we finished the classes, I believed Jon would not be the right team worker for troubled kids. I'd be left with sole responsibility for the children's disciplines and routines.

My father had been an orphan and in later years, after my mother had died, he stopped drinking and I learned to appreciate him. He promoted adoption and in honor of him, I agreed to visit Elizabeth and Raymond, ages four and three, when a social worker called. My dad had passed away only two months before Jon and I met the children. After we had gone the gamut of interviews, applications, and essays, I became confused. I scheduled a meeting in our home with the four social workers assigned to Elizabeth and Raymond's case. With Jon, we sat in the living room of our home. I openly questioned whether or not the children should be with us. Fearful that Jon would present me as incompetent, I explained my feelings about parenting with Jon.

I stated my case that I didn't know if our marriage would last, that Jon really had no knowledge about children. I had babysat from the time I was eleven years old. My nieces and nephews, now in their teens and twenties, had been constants in my life all through their childhoods. Yet, Jon convinced the social workers that we should adopt. His arguments included his having taught sixth grade, and because of that he apparently knew all about child development. Jon could manipulate anyone in the beginning of a relationship, as he had with me, and he did just that in that room by talking smoothly and believably.

The social workers never questioned my angst. In retrospect, I believe they wanted a home for the children so badly that they were willing to risk whatever might happen. As it turned out, I decided that Jon or no Jon, the children needed a home and I determined to give them just that.

At a later date, Jon would disclose his true motive to adopt. He surmised that I would not leave him if *I* had children. Vigorously involved in the children's lives when he admitted to this, I stowed his words, his gall, away in my subconscious. I had no time to address his attitude, yet his confession ate at me.

My father's voice from the past came to me. "It takes two to tangle," influencing the belief that I caused the marital rift, though Jon broke his promises. Elizabeth's and Raymond's early abandonment impacted my decision, as well. I worried the children would blame themselves if we split up.

Maintaining sensitivity to what the children had endured in early childhood while changing their attitudes required a delicate balance. They had different and more demanding needs than children born to and nurtured from birth by biological parents. My prophetic fear about parenting with Jon became truth. Jon, in denial that the children had been abused, refused to respect that I worked with and for foster and adoptive families, employment I had changed to after the children joined us. I understood that certain protocol should be followed to change the behavior of such abused children.

When the children first moved in, I told him we had to hide certain things, like matches and sentimental items, objects that naturally curious children will test. Jon pooh-poohed my caution. As such, Elizabeth lit a match to her bedding one day. Fortunately, the flame went out quickly. Another time, four-year-old Raymond broke a tool that had belonged to Jon's beloved grandfather. Jon related with an irritated voice that Raymond had broken it and he had ignored Jon's request not to touch the instrument. But Jon said nothing else about what had transpired, and the episode quickly escaped my mind, but only temporarily.

"Mom, my behind hurts to lie on it," Raymond told me that night as I sat on his bed to quiet him before sleep.

"Did you fall, Ray?"

"No."

"Well, lie on your side. I'm sure it'll feel better in the morning." I rubbed his little back.

After the children's weekly therapy sessions, the therapist habitually spent a few minutes with the parents alone. This particular week, her eyebrows furrowed, and she glared at me.

"Raymond says Jon made him strip and then hit him with a board. Are you aware of this?"

Aghast, I said, "No! Of course not." I shook my head. I knew a lot of things that Jon would and would not do, but this I found hard to accept.

"Talk to Raymond. It wouldn't be ethical for me to peer at his bottom, but perhaps he might show you."

That night, Raymond did show me his wounds of reds and blues. "Are you sure, Ray, that you didn't fall?" I looked into his brown eyes, hoping for another truth.

"No," he said with tears welled in his eyes. "Dad did that. He was mad at me. I didn't mean to break his tool."

When Jon insisted I sit at the table with him after the children had gone to bed, I broke his pattern of putting me on trial. I spoke first.

"Is it true that you spanked Raymond with a board?" I enunciated each word, carefully expressing disbelief. My face felt hot with suppressed anger. Thinking he would deny the accusation, I readied to tell him that this time there'd be no more staying, the children and I would leave.

Jon put his hands on his cheeks and bowed his head, failing to show his face. "Yes, I did. I don't know what came over me."

Once again, I accepted his remorse. I believed in the sincerity of his apology because when I got up from the table, he didn't pursue pressuring me to undergo the nightly evaluation.

After that, we agreed to talk about how to handle certain situations and to support each other with strategies. But, when I most depended upon him, he would undermine me. We agreed, for example, we should ignore Elizabeth during her screaming temper tantrums. But Jon would tell me with Elizabeth listening, that *I* was crazy, and that

Elizabeth had no troubles. Then he talked to her at length for an hour or more, heedlessly encouraging her shrillness to last longer.

Consequently, when I had to entrust the children to his care, I worried until they could be with me again. Home again, I questioned them about their day. Sometimes they tattled on Jon to play us against each other, as children will often do. Sometimes these recounts were noteworthy. Jon often tuned out, letting the children do as they pleased. As very little ones, they would wander the streets of the small town where we lived. That would have been okay, except the town lay immediately off an interstate. The social workers had cautioned us that a person from the children's past might try to kidnap them. When I would return home to find Elizabeth and Raymond unsupervised, I confronted Jon, who would twist the issue and taunt me.

One Saturday, the children painted with their watercolors on the back porch where I could see them from the kitchen. They began to argue and before I could get to them, they threw paint, which splattered over the newly hung curtains I had just made. I walked in, picked Elizabeth up from her chair that she gripped with her legs. When she let go, the chair dropped, causing a tremendous clanging.

Jon, puffing from hurrying to the scene, stood in the doorway. While Raymond and Elizabeth carried on with their argument, Jon accused me of having abused them. Dumbfounded, I said nothing. I did not want to lose my patience with Jon in the children's presence. Since I would not react, Jon disappeared. The incident died down and I had the children help me clean up the mess.

In the next therapist's visit, Jon said, demurely, that I abused the children and that it had been happening for some time. I angrily contradicted the claims, which turned the few minutes of parents' time into a free-for-all of unpleasant word slinging. For several visits thereafter, we verbally fought in the therapist's presence, until she urged us to attend marriage counseling. Jon would not work with a woman therapist, and we found only one male marriage counselor. After five sessions, I refused to attend. Jon talked about everything including his work, the weather, where he grew up, but not about the crucial issues. Exasperated with his avoidance, I quit. Nothing would stop him from accusing me of child abuse whenever I demanded appropriate behavior from the children. I began to feel humiliated and disconsolate.

At home, Jon closed himself frequently in his downstairs room to play computer games. He rarely talked to me. Together we attended Raymond's soccer games and both children's music recitals. I set up occasional outings for us, such as a movie and dinner, but Jon chose not to talk to me, nor to anyone else on our dates, not even to a waiter.

"Ok. Jon, you don't want to converse with me. Do you have anything you'd like to say?" I asked during one of our last dinners together. He regarded me as though I lived in some distant past and looked at me dubiously. He said nothing.

Meanwhile, no matter what Raymond did, whether it be yard work, homework, or piano playing, Jon found fault with him. Ray, an earnest child, had a meticulous manner about him. An artist in his heart, he did nothing sloppily.

Before meals at home, we held hands, taking turns saying a short prayer of thanks for our food. One night, Raymond, holding his palm up, took Jon's hand. Abruptly, with no apparent motive, Jon turned Raymond's hand over and smacked it down on the table. Imagining Raymond's pain, I yelled, "That was completely uncalled for." In tears, Raymond jerked his hand away, shoved his chair out from the table and ran to his room in the downstairs walkout. I followed him. He rolled underwear, a t-shirt, and his toothbrush into a bandana. He was only eleven years old, and in a few months, he would die.

Jon shouted from the top of the steps, "If you hadn't said anything, he wouldn't have reacted."

"Raymond, it's not a good idea for you to go. Stay and we'll work this out." I said as tears clouded my sight.

"I can't stand this anymore Mom! Dad has to control everything that I do. He's like the white men that beat down the African Americans. He's mean." Being biracial, Raymond had an avid interest in history and the treatment of people of color. Bent over his travel baggage, his tears wet the cloth, causing the red in its pattern to deepen into crimson. "I'm leaving," he exclaimed, pounding his feet up the stairs and out the front door, carrying his hobo bag.

Jon stood in the kitchen watching Raymond go. "I don't know what makes me so mean," he said coyly, as though expecting me to answer.

I pointed to the door. "Follow him. You're the one who needs to bring him home," I said as my voice cracked.

Raymond, walking the gravel roads, had already disappeared, heading toward the Cedar River less than a mile away. Jon cut through the pastures to catch up. In silence, Elizabeth and I watched from the yard. I could feel Raymond's pull to the water, to throw his anger to the current. If only I could have done the same.

Within an hour, Jon and Ray walked toward home on the road, side by side. Raymond, tall and slim, carrying his pack. Jon's shoulders bent. In the distance, I could see Jon's legs working hard to match Raymond's long-legged stride. When they reached us, Raymond giggled and said, "That was a good workout." Jon, breathing heavily, wiped the sweat from his brow. I would never know what words they had exchanged. Raymond, an optimist, did not hold grudges, so I knew by his lighthearted comment he had forgiven Jon.

Yet, Jon continued to exhibit sullen behavior. Frequently, I asked him to make an appointment with a doctor, knowing that physical ailments can cause ill temper, though he had always been churlish to some degree. Each time I asked, he shrugged his shoulders. Nevertheless, when Raymond ran away, my resolve to continue trying within the marriage died. Raymond's comment regarding the treatment of African Americans struck a chord. Worn down as I had become, I understood how dominance can destroy a feisty spirit.

Deeply concerned that our home life would leave more scars on the children, I had to liberate us. In order to leave, though, I needed to find full-time employment. I would need to find after-school care, should a job not allow me to be home. We had dogs, cats, and horses that needed to remain with the children and me. As Christmas 2003 swiftly approached, I vowed to make that holiday the best ever by decorating, baking cookies, and hosting family and friends. Jon obliged by stringing outside lights on the house eaves. I concluded that I would figure out how to leave him after the holidays.

My intention would not be carried through, however. On December 14th, the day of Elizabeth's and Raymond's first joint recital of violin and piano, the four of us rode in the van. It would be our last ride together. At approximately 1:00 p.m., the semi hit us.

In the days, weeks and months following the accident, my head injuries and PTSD caused obsessive thoughts, fatigue, confusion, headaches, and varied sleep patterns. Either I wanted to sleep a lot, or I couldn't at all. I cried often, even over insignificant matters. Certain words eluded me when I talked, and I had no memory of movies and books I had read during my life. Memories of things I had done with friends or family over the years deserted me. I feared people would find me strange and incompetent. I did odd things. For example, even though I gave away Jon's clothes, I kept his shoes thinking he might return and need them. I did not want to be perceived as mean, leaving him barefoot.

Later, as my mind settled and began healing, it occurred to me Jon had always been barefoot so to speak, as he never had anything solid to stand on. In turbulent times, his mother had kept him afloat. When I came along, he expected me to sustain him, but I demanded he put on work boots and dig in. Lacking tenacity, not knowing how to hold himself up, he tore at me.

The clairvoyant said Jon stood at the mailbox, that he wanted a message delivered to me. Even in death, he could not face life nor me. Throughout our time together, I had sensed his fear, and like a wild animal hearing a roaring river, I kept a distance. I could say I stayed with him for the children's sake. In essence, since he could not take care of himself, I would have forever blamed myself if he had drowned.

CHAPTER
Five

PASSING THROUGH

Two springs before Raymond and Jon died, I'm in the middle of a phone call when Raymond and Elizabeth clomp down the stairs. They thud into my basement office on a hot April day, declaring that Demetra, one of our dogs, has cornered a snake by the garage. Certain of its species—prairie rattler—they fret that it will bite and kill Demetra. I follow them, though dubious about the name. I'm hoping it's not a timber rattlesnake, which are venomous and do exist in Iowa.

At an outside corner of the garage, Demetra hops back and forth, snarling, pokes her muzzle toward a coiled and hissing black and brown-patterned serpent. Our other dog, Sasha, keeps his distance. I grab Demetra's collar and pull, drag her into the house, and tell the children to move away to let the snake calm down.

The three of us stand, watching it. Slowly it uncurls, stretches out, slicks along with a seemingly unending length. I want to fly up to the rooftop, to be as far from the creature as possible. But it fascinates me. Its ringed tail rattles like toothpicks clinking in a tin container. After we lose sight of it, I grab the opportunity for a family research project.

Children and dogs pile into the van and ride with me to the public library, which Jon directs. The dogs, on leashes, pull us into the building. We trip over each other's legs in our hurry to gather information.

"Dad! Dad!" Raymond is the first in, describing the snake.

"A prairie rattler," Elizabeth adds, "his tail made that sound!"

On the computer, Jon googles Iowa reptiles and photos appear on the screen.

The children and I simultaneously zero in on a body that's brown and black-patterned with creamy undertones and a particularly small head.

"Fox snake! That's it!" Raymond exclaims.

Elaphe vulpina, otherwise known as the fox snake, has the distinguishing feature of a faux rattle, built-in protection to fool predators. It appears to be poisonous. However, it has no venom. Like most snakes, it prefers staying close to the earth, not dangling from trees, and it does adapt to human habitat, though it favors covertness, hence the name fox. This species shows minimal aggression. Typically, they move away from commotion rather than confront it, but they will strike and bite if provoked. They also constrict their prey.

Back home, the children and I walk alertly when outside. I become more attentive to the dogs' barking, thinking when I hear them that they've cornered another snake. One afternoon, while supervising Elizabeth practicing the violin and Raymond practicing the piano, I look out the window and by chance see two young fox snakes mating in the grass. At first glance, the snakes seem tied together in a knot. But, as I focus in more closely, I see they wiggle slightly from side to side, gracefully and slowly turning. I glimpse the pale yellow of their undersides.

These must be fox snakes, I assume, because these have a faint pattern of brown. With age, most snakes become more intense in color. I call the children over to watch. Raymond immediately opens the sliding door to go out for a closer view.

"No Ray, leave them be," I say. "It's a private thing and if you disturb them, they'll not have any eggs for baby snakes."

"But Mom."

We turn back to our viewing place and find no snakes.

"Did you see them leave, Elizabeth?"

"No, and I was looking."

Summertime, two years after the vehicular accident that took Jon and Raymond's lives, I sit cross-legged on the living room rug with a deck of *Medicine Cards*, a Native American prophetic inquiry, in hand. Sun, high in the west, gives full light, makes the house hotter than need be, but sun delivers life. My heart requires its energy now more than ever.

No amount of reading, nor of going to therapy has released me from the cold, hard underworld of grief. I serve on the school board, co-teach NAMI (National Alliance on Mental Illness) classes, help with the local animal shelter, remain active in Elizabeth's life, and keep up friendships. But I have two parts. One, the social side with functions and commitments. The other part has no movement. It stays dormant, eludes comfort and fulfillment. It also insists upon accepting numbness and it hides.

I seek answers to fuse my two broken selves into one whole being. I close my eyes and meditate on the peacefulness of my environment. In the immediate outside, a wren chirps. A mile or so away, I hear a truck's wheels crunching the gravel, speeding along. I settle in, let my muscles relax as the sounds fade into the background.

Since the December afternoon when our vehicle folded up like a paper box at the semi's impact, bizarre impositions have plagued me. Amongst them snake encounters, which are more persistent than when Raymond lived, and have driven me to pull the *Medicine Cards* from my bookshelves. I shuffle the deck and trust the animal that reveals itself, an ally, will allow me some insight. I shift the position of my legs to make myself comfortable. I take a deep breath and slip my fingers in-between the cards. I grab a card and flip it over. The illustration of a viper faces me. Its body curves into four loops, the way a snake poses when semi-relaxed. This one has wound herself around her eggs. Her ringed tail and heart-shaped head flaunt tenacity. Portrayed as insulating her young, she pulls on my maternal instincts, on my need to protect Elizabeth, and my despair of not having kept Raymond from harm.

Despite that, I hadn't expected a snake. My body gives a little shudder and I let the card drop, face up, from my hand. A time did exist when seeing a photo or an illustration of a snake would have sent chills coursing through me and made me scream. But, as I have had several significant exposures to real ones, I *am* getting used to viewing these silent and enigmatic creatures.

The spring after Raymond and Jon died, my friends, Mike and Ruth, tilled a ten-by-fourteen foot space for a garden at my place. They carefully pounded in steel posts and stretched horse fencing, then lined it with chicken wire to deter deer, raccoons, and other smaller pilferers. Still not up to doing strenuous physical work, I thanked Mike and Ruth profusely. They'd reap most of the produce at harvest, but the growing vegetation became a constant reminder that moving forward would put months, and eventually years, between the accident and my memory. That distance in time pointed to healing. For some months, friends and neighbors like Mike and Ruth continued to help Elizabeth and me. The community opened its arms and wrapped us up. New friends evolved from people I once knew as acquaintances.

One morning, a friend dropped off a flat of strawberry cuttings. Mike and Ruth, already at work, spent extra time setting the young plants into rows. Summer passed and the plants merely established themselves but did not produce fruit that first season. September arrived. In spite of all the help I'd received, with the harvest now in, I concluded that I would never again have the stamina to labor in the garden. I unhooked the wire. The next day, I wiggled a post until it pulled easily from the earth. I took out one post per day until all the fencing materials lined up against the wall inside the shop. My brain, still in tumult, grasped only the apparent fact that my body felt beaten and broken. It never occurred to me that I had destroyed Mike and Ruth's arduously built fence, or that I might need the enclosure.

The following June, strawberry vegetation stood upright, dark green leaves and spreading tentacles dotted with blooms. I watched the fruits grow bigger and riper and waited with anticipation to pluck the berries.

Finally, colander in hand, ready to reap the first batch, I spotted mature ones half-eaten. Birds? Raccoons? I needed to figure out some way to protect the strawberries. In the shop, I found short posts, three feet high, that had been left from some other time. I pressed them into the ground still soft from spring rains. I threw bird netting over the top of the posts, forming an open-air tent. My soft cage spread over the six-by-five-foot patch and, though lopsided, it appeared practical. Job done. Devising the shelter hadn't taken much energy and standing over it with arms crossed, I smiled.

Two days later, the netting had fallen and the plants blanketed with reddened strawberries had bruised leaves and broken stems. Reaching under my ingenious contraption, I gently pulled the greenery free. Birds chirped, swooping closely by, and the breeze whooshed. All else remained quiet. As I released the fruits, my thoughts turned to picking cherries and apples on the farm where I grew up. Memories of climbing the trees, hanging on the limbs, and eating more than I put in the pail transferred me back in time. While the flashback played, my ears registered a rattling, snapping me back to the present just as my fingers brushed against something that felt calloused, and unfamiliar.

I shivered. I stood up. I paced. I returned to peer at the forms that looked as though they had been mating, the way they lay rolled together. Now they barely moved. With my eyes, I followed the tangle of brown and cream patterns through the foliage and found tails. I followed the curved lines in the opposite direction to see small, flat heads ensnared tightly in the webbing.

I reached out, daring to touch them but they hissed, and my arm, suddenly an entity of its own, flapped back to my side. The bodies wove in and out through the patch and, noting that, my legs jittered. With snakes there, I couldn't finish what I had set out to do. I wondered if I should bang them over their heads and put them out of their misery? They would never escape their entanglement. Whatever decision I made, to free them or not, would prove their fate. No, I couldn't kill them. I couldn't even kill a spider in my house.

I stepped this way and that, observing the patch from all angles.

Back in the house, Elizabeth watched TV and for the slightest moment I thought of asking her for help. Raymond would have been excited to help release the snakes. But with Elizabeth, the mildest answer I could hope for would be a "NO!"

I could have left the snakes to their own destiny. But I knew they'd eventually expire. Though their presence spooked me, I couldn't allow them to die, these creatures of the earth. On a concrete level, I had come to appreciate the snakes as part of life's chain. They eat vermin and insects and fertilize the soil. Owning a deed to land gives me no rights in nature, though it offers a habitat in which to design my own harmony, regulate my own circumstances. Nature also entitles me to witness transmutations of a Superior Being, which many call God.

I decided to call Mary and Dan, my nearest neighbors, whom I depended upon when absolutely stuck, which unfortunately, occurred often. Mary had taught Raymond and Elizabeth in third grade, finding humor in their sometimes-mischievous attitudes. Dan had little spare time, but if I needed his help, he fixed things that I could not.

On the phone, I said, "Mary, do you have any savvy about snakes?"

"No," she said in a voice that indicated I asked more than what she wanted to consider. "But Dan's here. I'll send him over."

I stopped by the TV long enough to tell Elizabeth to come and watch the untangling of snakes.

"Not on your life!" She yelled.

Dan arrived, driving a lawn mower and pulling an open wagon behind it filled with his and Mary's children: Ashley, a high school student, and Bridget and Jack, yet to begin school. Mary walked behind.

"My assistants," Dan said lightheartedly as everybody jumped out of the wagon.

I took them to the patch. Hovering my finger above the bodies, I traced them in the air. Dan pulled scissors from his pocket, cut the netting around the snakes to a much smaller portion, grabbed the creatures from behind their heads and pulled them up, still tightly entangled.

Dan set them in the wagon while Ashley held the snakes and stretched each one out, her blonde hair dangling within inches of the extended bodies. Dan carefully cut close in. The snakes didn't hiss, wiggle, or rattle. Bridget and Jack watched intently, leaning up against the wagon. Mary and I kept a sizeable distance, breathing shallowly, standing completely still.

After some time, Dan held up a freed snake, stretching his arm out from his side. The tail dangled to his ankle, showing a length of five feet or more. These reptiles' diameters equaled about the size of two rake handles stuck together. Ashley took the snake from him, released it into the ditch. One done. Dan and Ashley carefully unsnagged the second one. Within an hour after my rescuers arrived, both serpents recouped their freedom.

At the time, I didn't allow myself much distance on the episode. Like everything during that time of despair, it left me with yet another obsessive anxiety.

Each day, I walked out to the strawberry patch. I stood over it. The berries ripened. The birds came and ate them. I could see raccoon tracks in and around the area. In the nights, the wild animals had their fill. Berries, over-ripened then fell. Red spreads underneath the plants.

"I must go out and pick the berries," I said to myself, colander in hand, on several days, yet not making it out to the garden.

Slowly, I regained my composure. At first, close to the patch, I would look carefully, surveying each leaf, each stem. Without leaning further in, or using my hands to probe, I would scan, my eyes closer to the earth. Then, cautiously, I would set my knees to the ground. Finally, when satisfied that nothing but berry plants existed, I would stretch out a hand and pick, but not without presuming I might see another snake. Every time I reached into the greenery, I hesitated.

Each time I went to the small area, I began to notice things I hadn't previously taken the time to regard. A small black spider stretched its web, dewed and glistening, between one plant and another. It hung in the middle of the lacy strands, master of its domain, waiting for a fly, a beetle, any small bug to entrap itself and become a breakfast catch.

A cardinal landed within six feet of me one morning as I balanced on one knee. Unfazed by my presence, it poked its head in and then out, as birds do, its beak in the grass. Soon, it snatched a cricket and rose from the ground effortlessly, black legs dangling from its bill. It flew to where the bird feeder swayed with the breeze and, for a moment, joined its mate and sang before both flew away.

Another time, a skunk wandered into the yard. Knowing that skunks eat fruit, I held myself as still as possible, hoping it would not join me in the berry patch. The skunk had an itinerary, digging where the earth undulated from the tunneling voles. That day I quietly slipped away to the house and did not stay to witness the outcome.

Almost every day some creature revealed an activity of its life. I realized that each had a mode of survival. No matter what an animal might face in its life, it had a purpose: it fed itself and its family. The animals responded to daily situations as needs arose. I doubted they dreamt up hypothetical threats, or worried neurotically, as were my inclinations.

After the accident, I had tortured myself, rehashing the morning before our accident. I repeatedly asked myself: *What if we'd done this instead of that?* In my mind, I refigured each detail before getting in the van and leaving on that fateful day. I fixed the timing, changed the outcome. Each time I relived the scenes, new anxieties smacked me. Elizabeth carried her own misery, which had also disturbed my soul. I needed to accept that what had been done was done. No amount of willing could change it. It came to me, then, that I had to confront whatever trials might arise instead of running away.

Now, from where I sit on the floor, I open the book that accompanies the *Medicine Cards*. I read, "The transmutation of the life-death-rebirth cycle is exemplified by the shedding of Snake's skin. It is the energy of wholeness, cosmic consciousness, and the ability to experience anything willingly and without resistance..."

The fox snakes my neighbors released didn't show themselves again that summer. The largest bull snakes, king snakes, garter snakes, and racers I'd ever dreamt possible did appear. All these ophidians I spotted while I drove the riding lawn mower. To my relief, I had no ground contact with them. I could regard them aloofly. However, some of these critters slipped away from the big machine's vibrations right into holes in my vegetable and flower gardens. Holes that, until then, I hadn't realized belonged to them. Holes like the metaphorical ones that I sought refuge in.

These quiet creatures, snakes, harbingers of the underground, appeared more abundantly after I delved within, intending to conceal my fears and sadness from others, and, most of all, from myself. I do my best thinking, touch deeply into my emotions when in a natural silence, like that of St. Joe's cemetery, which carries the sound of wind, birds, and coyotes at night. This dormant half of me moves along in its own realm, dodging for an inner place when insecurity hits, when my comfort level among people diminishes. When I anticipate having to answer questions about my family.

I continue reading from the *Medicine Cards* booklet, "the knowledge that all things are equal in creation, and that those things which might be experienced as poison can be eaten, ingested, integrated, and transmuted, if one has the proper state of mind."

Information new to me since the accident doesn't store easily. The head trauma I sustained obliterated certain aspects of my memories. However, conversation and reading tend to trigger and restore forgotten knowledge. Seeing certain objects jiggles my recall, too.

On my early morning walk down the gravel road, not long after the rescue of the fox snakes, a bull snake crossed a few feet in front of me. I stopped dead fast, veins pulsing beneath my skin, the black and grey pattern of the snake alarming amongst the browns and greens of a roadside background. Bull snakes can be aggressive. This one, though, went hurriedly on its way but not without swirling a cloud in my brain, tapping an almost forgotten episode.

On an April morning four months after the accident, I had opened the overhead garage door to see a snake racing down the lane, its body curving in and out at an incredible speed. Aimed in my direction, I noted its good size. I'd rather have retreated into the house, but I grabbed a rake, thinking that I'd swoop up the serpent, carry it out to the road, shake it off and dump it. I meant it no harm. I needed to take charge. I needed to prove to myself I could live alone in the country.

Acting quickly, I placed the rake tines on the ground, as a stop sign. Snakes don't know about stop signs, though. It climbed on, not missing a beat, wound around, continuing on, covering the handle and weighing it down, moving toward my hands, my face. Despite my physical pain and the injuries that yet needed to heal, I mustered all my might and threw the rake, landing it near the front porch. The snake, a fox snake (I got a good, close-up look and recalled it well), sunk like water down a drain into the hole at the southwest corner of the house faster than I could emit a scream.

Fear of being bitten and facing my demise by constriction unleashed a kneejerk response of survival. Kneejerk, that's what I do when I'm threatened. Rather than allowing myself that burrowing time for observation, time to inhale and exhale deeply to savor the moments, I rush. I deny my innate self. I ignore what my soul intuits.

Every person must make choices. I can take the horror I've been handed and face it to the sun. Fire it. Let it grow anew. I've been given a new life, a different life. I needed to penetrate the apathetic barrier, to warm up, to keep my mood above ground, out of the pit. I do have two parts and one balances the other, should I allow them to work in unison.

By demanding courage from me, these creatures have led me to an awakening. The fox snake climbing my rake signaled a passing through. After weeks of physical and emotional impairment, I finally had strength to defend myself. At the time, though, I had yet to recognize that my old skin had been shed.

CHAPTER

Six

COYOTE TALES

I grab the vial of Trazodone from the counter. Empty.

Elizabeth nods, looks at me. The whites of her eyes show like the coyote that my neighbor caught and stuck in a cage. Her chin has that insolent tilt to it that says, "I'll show you."

Three days ago, Elizabeth's doctor prescribed the pills.

"I took them all," she says and holds the phone out to me. She's talking to her friend's mom, whom she called instead of me. Her shoulders bend forward, her body slumps a little. "Here, talk to Alex's mom," she tells me.

I grab the phone and hang up, then dial 911. My knees tremble. I want to shake Elizabeth, then myself, each for different reasons.

The woman on the other end tells me the emergency crew will arrive in 10 to 15 minutes.

"What do I do? Do I have her sit? Lie down? Walk?" I pace back and forth, a cornered wolf.

"I can't tell you that," the voice says, "I'm not trained to give advice."

Elizabeth is stumbling now. She teeters down the front hall to the closet, puts on her coat, her shoes, and sits in the chair there. I can't talk, try to retain my composure. I hook Ella, my dog, to her leash, anticipating the coming confusion. I look out the window and see a man jump from his truck, run to open the gate to our country lane in time for a fire truck, a pickup, and an ambulance to rush through. Just as quickly, several men file through the front door carrying an oxygen mask and other paraphernalia.

Elizabeth is slurring her words. Her head sits at an angle and rolls back and forth mechanically. "We've never had to deal with an overdose," one man says. Time is of the essence to prevent Elizabeth from having permanent brain damage, another tells me. The closest hospital is 30 miles away. Elizabeth opens her mouth and vomit spews out, flowing over her, landing on the men, the chair, the floor. One man picks her up and carries her to the ambulance. "I'll be right behind you," I say to the last one out.

I grab my purse and think to grab clean clothes for Elizabeth. Ella jumps in the car, rides shotgun. The man shutting the gate behind us calls out, "Good luck."

On the road, I call Mike and Ruth, unfailing friends. As I begin to speak, it comes to me that those men would've been the very ones who'd pulled us out of our crushed van on I-80 two years ago, when Jon and Raymond died, and Elizabeth and I barely made it out. This thought breaks me, but I manage to say, "Elizabeth is on the way to the hospital," before I begin to sob. We make a plan: Mike and Ruth meet me halfway to Iowa City. Ruth gets in the car with me, and Mike takes Ella.

On chilly, clear-skied evenings here in rural Iowa, coyote songs are frequent. From across the pastures, the harmonies carry. The music takes me far from civilization and transforms the chaos of my life into a new story, a sweet story where wildlife watch over me and humans can't judge me. Some mornings I've found scat in front of the garage or on the back patio, though I've yet to see the coyote. She's elusive.

These "leavings" make me wonder: Are they a sign of what my life has become? Or does Coyote sense my oblivion, sense that I need a strong awakening? Of course, Coyote doesn't know anything about me, but I believe that by hanging so close in, she breathes a message. What's she up to, what would she tell me, if she could? Would she soothe Elizabeth and me, ease our pain?

We are a family unit, sitting at the supper table. The table has a comfortable fit in the small kitchen, but when all four of us sit around it to share a meal, it feels crowded.

"Hey Sissy," Raymond says. "Ish ke aw wan ran ve di ovey ord."

"Sheek! Ick aud veem aw di ovey ord!" Elizabeth responds in their gibberish, and both she and Raymond shriek.

"Hey," I instruct, "that's not the tone of voice to use at the dinner table." Elizabeth doesn't bother to look at me, nor at Jon, but concentrates on Raymond, continuing in their made-up language.

"Joink doy!" Ray giggles, "They don't know!" He holds his fork toward the middle of the table and before I can say anything, Elizabeth has met his reach with hers. Jon says nothing, just continues eating.

Now both children are screaming "Eeeeee" at the top of their lungs. The dogs start barking and I jump in my seat.

Finally, Jon reacts, "That's enough!" But his words don't stop them.

"Hoy doit!" Raymond giggles. Elizabeth screams again.

I jump up and pull out her chair. "Supper's over for you two."

Elizabeth screams, then cries. I take her to the time-out chair. She's only six, yet she knows how to shred my inner calm as if it were a piece of paper. "Stay there," I say to her. But she screams nonstop. I try to ignore her and go back to the table. "You need to go to bed," I tell Raymond.

"No way," he exclaims like a teenager, though he's only five. "Now!" I go to pull out his chair, but he's off it and running away from me. Jon, sitting, says, "Can't you control them?"

Elizabeth likes that Jon won't back me. Consequently, she screams louder.

"It's Trumpleton, Mom," Ray tells me later when I'm tucking him in. "It's our language. It's just me and Elizabeth when we talk that. We belong to each other. She's my sister and she's my favorite friend in the whole world," he says. His little body lies still, and he looks straight at me, his big brown eyes intent on his thoughts.

"Perhaps," I say to Elizabeth as I tuck her in, "you could speak Trumpleton somewhere besides at the supper table."

"No! Raymond and I need to talk, and you don't need to know what we're saying."

"Fine," I say, "just not at the supper table."

The next night at dinner, Elizabeth says to Raymond, "It's you and me against them."

"Oyi det midt fhet sa," Raymond says and looks at me. His brown eyes filled with laughter.

I take a big breath and let it out slowly, look past them. "How was your day, Jon?"

We lived in a small town when a social worker dropped off Elizabeth (age five) and Raymond (age four) on a stifling Iowa summer evening. Each carried one grocery bag of belongings. They dropped their bags and immediately ran around the house, out the door and in the door, several times, banging it behind them with each turnabout.

The cats hid and the dogs ran. I opened the back door, scooting the dogs out, and the children swept along with them, dug their toes in the chain link fence, trying to climb the six feet.

Jon rallied them to return to the house, where he encouraged them to open a box that his mom had sent. Papers wrapped around toys flew to the floor, the children's hands and arms windmills of excitement. That accomplished, they ran through the house from one room to the next, laughing loudly and shrilly.

The social worker said, "I hope that these kids will be able to form an attachment. I should have brought you and Jon a bottle of bourbon." Then she left.

A few months after the children arrived, I hired on as a research specialist for Iowa Foster and Adoptive Parents Association. There, I learned things that hadn't been mentioned in the mandatory classes given by Human Services for prospective adoptive parents. Children who don't know how to bond may never bond with anyone, I found out. For some, if trust didn't exist in early childhood, it may never form. These kids, defiant by learned behavior, have what's called Radical Attachment Disorder (RAD), in other words, a fear of emotional connections. The adult who sticks with a child, who loves and believes in her, instigates the worst behaviors, as the child fights to keep from being loved. For the same reason, the child might also strive to break up a good rapport between other people close to her. At that point, the concept of RAD challenged me. Where another person might have feared or dreaded what could transpire with Elizabeth's and Raymond's personalities, I chose not to label them. Instead, I made up my mind to do the best I could to teach them about love and trust.

A couple of years passed. We moved to the country, where more dogs and a horse joined our family. Raymond's rapport with the animals may have helped him mature enough to resist Elizabeth's antics. Yet Elizabeth continued to think of stunts, always drawing attention to her, and these actions continued to cause unrest within our family.

"Mom, Elizabeth made fun of me in school today," Raymond confided to me one night shortly before bedtime, the time I took to share with each child alone. On his side in bed, he propped his head up on one hand.

"What did she do this time, Ray?" I bit my lip, braced myself.

"She called me a dirty name, the N-word in front of my friends. And the guys who hate me were right behind me. She knew it, too. I think that's why she did it, because then they started in and said nasty things to me." Tears welled into Raymond's eyes and his voice shook as he said this. In fourth grade now, he didn't cry as easily as he once had.

I sighed. "I'm sorry, Ray." I gently rubbed my thumb on his forehead. "Do you know what may have caused her to do that?" Elizabeth taunting Raymond had become a pattern, a result of his not agreeing to her next plotting.

"Yeah. I think it's because I told her I didn't want to skip school." His tears dripped onto the pillow.

I wanted to cry with him, but I held it in. Raymond's sadness made my whole body well up like a flooded river. "You did the right thing, Ray. I'll talk to her. Tell the therapist at our next session."

"But Mom! Why does she do this to me? She's my sister and she makes me feel so awful!" He turned on his back, his face contorted from the emotional pain.

"I don't know. I wish I knew." I gave him a tight hug and told him a story about Sasha. As a young-adopted dog, he started biting viciously, but disciplining him and giving him pets and biscuits, brushing him when he acted the "good" dog, molded him into the lovable guy that the children knew.

Raymond chuckled and said, "Sasha is a good dog."

In Elizabeth's room, I sat on her bed. She scrunched up in a fetal position. I put my hand on her forehead to relax her. She pushed me away.

"Raymond feels really bad. He says you said some nasty things to him at school," I said this calmly while leaning back against the wall. My feet dangled over the side of the bed.

"I don't know what he's talking about," she said, and pulled the covers up over her head.

"OK. If you don't, then I guess you don't. But I think you do." After a bit, I said, "Raymond loves you dearly." Then, I told her the story of Sasha, the same story I had told Raymond. When I finished, she threw the covers off, and abruptly sat up.

"I hate Sasha," she screamed in my ear.

Raymond, the only person in the world Elizabeth trusts, leaves this life at eleven years old. Two months later Elizabeth's thirteenth birthday follows, where upon she conveys the condition of her soul: Deep. Huge.

Vacant. Pocked with sorrow from early and unresolved abuses and overwhelming losses, she believes herself unworthy of any good. And now she must contend with the deaths of her father and her brother.

Rage conducts Elizabeth. She uses it to conceal a heart pummeled early on by ignorant and sometimes mean grown-ups and to mask her most recent losses. To Elizabeth, someone must be accountable. One adult remains. She smacks the big letter A on me: "Accused."

I, too, feel the anger, the wrath of being left alone to deal with her troubles, and the umbrage of the physical injuries from the accident that continue to impair me. Most of all, though, I bear the fierce emotional pain that both Elizabeth and I suffer from not being able to watch Raymond grow up.

Ruth and I find our way to the emergency room, where Alex's mom stands over Elizabeth's gurney. Somehow, she's arrived before I could get here. Elizabeth, sitting up in bed, ignores me. A nurse holds out a concoction of charcoal.

"I don't need that now," Elizabeth says, waving her away. "I puked at home and in the ambulance."

"Drink it all. No cheating. It'll soak up any of the drug left in your stomach," the nurse demands, putting the cup in front of Elizabeth's face.

I bite my lip and realize how my teeth and jaw hurt from clenching them.

"I was certain that you'd bring Elizabeth to this hospital, so I came immediately after I talked to her on the phone," Alex's mom says to me.

"Thank you for being here," I respond. I want to be civil to her but know that she can't understand the complexity of Elizabeth's and my relationship—not even I can figure it out. Still, I'm envious of her as her teenage daughter, Alex, can be a brat, but she responds to reason and she does normal things. She babysits, joins clubs at school, even talks with her mom. Elizabeth treats Alex's mom like a goddess when

I'm around. I hate it. I despise it because she treats me as though I should have died in that accident.

Ever faithful, Ruth, standing next to me, gives me a look that tells me she sees it all and she observes how uninformed the other mom is. Ruth understands my feelings, which I'm sure are splayed in the posture of my body and the look on my face. Ruth also comprehends how Elizabeth acts toward me, and her dramatic, polarizing appeal to Alex's mom.

"I'll be in the waiting room," Ruth says, offering the other mom a hint.

Alex's mom says she'll leave now that I'm here.

I sit with Elizabeth, but neither of us talk. When a doctor finally comes much later, he tells me that he wants to talk with my daughter first. I have to oblige, though I'd give anything to hear what they say. My neck muscles tense up. I'm concerned she might tell him that I've hit her. She has accused me of child abuse in the past, bringing officials into our lives. The investigation proved only that she had lied, but it left me feeling ashamed.

When I go to the waiting room, Alex's mom sits with her new boyfriend, their hands entwined. Her public display of affection for this guy makes me uncomfortable, probably because Jon and I didn't appreciate each other, and didn't show tenderness in our marriage. I also don't like it that she hangs around when she said she'd go home. I do appreciate her caring, but I also know what a pawn she is in Elizabeth's mind.

"You can go," I say. "Really, it's OK. I thank you for coming to help."

Each adoption expert that I consult about Elizabeth tells me the same thing: "She has RAD." As a result, her young mind formed on the basis of survival, instead of nurture. Small actions, things I wouldn't give a second thought to, could trigger a memory, set off a flight or fight response. The adults in the RAD child's early life might simply neglect her, or beat her, or even worse. Immediately after such heinous treatment, such an adult might give a handout such as a hug, smile, sweet treat as an offering of love. And the child learns not to trust it. Elizabeth learned to fend for herself, to become a mother for younger siblings, and to distrust all adults. Insisting that the world owes her something, she uses aggression to get what she wants. She might steal, hit, lie, manipulate, and feign love. Like Coyote, she becomes a trickster in order to survive.

In urban areas where housing developments infringe on wildlife habitats, some people chase coyotes and shoot at them. But others put out dog, cat, or human food, thinking they're doing Coyote a favor by offering her food. Coyote adapts to the feedings and comes to expect the offered meals. Then she gets angry and controlling when denied what she's come to anticipate. For her, the aggression is self-protection. It's survival. The RAD child gets contentious when she doesn't get what she wants and even when she does get it. She and Coyote run parallel.

When the doctor beckons me back from the waiting room, he takes me into an office and says, "We don't take overdoses lightly. Has your daughter ever threatened suicide before?" He sits behind a desk, which makes me feel as though I'm on trial.

"No. But she has threatened to kill me. Several times."

"How does she give these threats? Is she calm? Outraged? What's the scenario behind them?" His hands are folded, his elbows propped on the desk.

"Always in an outrage. Beyond reason. Sometimes she kicks violently at the doors that I close to keep us apart." I scratch my head, fold and unfold my hands, things that I do when I'm anxious. I want to tell him about the night before when she broke a glass and left the shards all over the kitchen table, strewn across the floor. How I swept it up and when I returned to the room maybe ten minutes later, a big chunk that I had swept up again lay on the floor. And I'm thinking about earlier in this day. As a New Year's present and a hope for new beginnings, I had signed us up for a mother-daughter dog-sled trip. We were to leave this next day, but Elizabeth refused to pack. Instead, she sat in her room brooding and ripping up her stuffed animals, her clothes, her papers. So, I began packing for both of us. I wanted to get us out of our environment, to be in the company of other mothers and daughters, to be in the wild. Taking Elizabeth into an uninhabited environment, to interact with dogs and with other girls her age, would be a healthy diversion. Or, so I thought.

"Elizabeth, how about this shirt? Is this comfortable for you? Something you'd like to take along?" I went to her room several times, asking her such questions, hoping to get her to break out of her mood and to talk. But she wouldn't answer me. Sometimes she wandered the room talking to herself. I pondered whether or not to call her therapist, but I felt defeated; her therapist had never believed anything I said. Elizabeth had bluffed every therapist I'd taken her to since she'd been a little girl.

Then I saw that she had drawn in ink on the fabric of her vanity bench. Furniture handed down in our family that had been in perfect condition. "You've got to pay attention to what you do. Your aunt gave this to you," I said this kindly, despite my exasperation. She sat on her bed and I stood over the bench. I felt my shoulders tighten, my breath quicken.

Her hair hadn't been brushed for days, stuck out, fell in her face. Her eyes peered out from underneath the mop. "You fucking bitch! I hate you. You're just a spoiled rotten fucking bitch! Get out of my room and stay out!" She came off the bed like a wild animal, leaping at me so quickly that we entangled, pushing and shoving at each other. She hit me in the arm and I grabbed the door, pushing it between us so I could get out.

"You hurt me!" She bellowed. I heard the bam, wonk, thunk, whap of things being thrown at her door, at her walls, and the continual yawp of a mad and injured animal. Frenzied, I turned toward her door to yell back, something I had done in past times. But this time I stopped, stepped back, took myself to the outside, headed toward the field where Sassy, our horse grazed. Being around Sassy, taking care of her, was a way to calm me, and I spent twenty minutes with her. When

I came back inside, Elizabeth had the phone in her hand and the prescription vial sat on the counter.

I want to tell the doctor all these things, but I fear he'll think my parenting skills unfit, that he'll want to know why I hadn't gone for help. Therapists have shattered my hopes when they have said things, such as, "You're the one with the problem, not Elizabeth." I don't want to rely on friends, either. I have called on them so many times since the accident, way too many times, I feel. Albeit they tell me they're on call, if I need them.

"When did these things start?" The doctor peers at me, studying me.

I focus on his hazel eyes behind the glasses. "She's always been a difficult child, but our lives became more complicated when her dad and brother were killed…" I trail off, not sure if I should tell him more and be more explicit. Not sure I want to get into it, I sit back and let out a big sigh.

"Well, I recommend that your daughter go to a psychiatric facility for testing. We don't have one here, so she'll have to be transported to University Hospitals. They'll probably keep her for at least three days." He stands up and the hem of his white coat touches the desktop.

I sit still. "Is she going by hospital transportation? How does she get there? And when?" I'm twisting in my chair to keep my eyes on him as he opens the door to show me the way out.

"You'll have to transport her." His foot braces open the door in a way that suggests I should move along.

I slump further into the chair. I can only imagine how she'll react to this. "Are you going to break the news to her?" And, then I think to say, "Please. Please talk to her." He nods and walks ahead of me into the curtained-off emergency room cubby.

"That charcoal stuff was awful," Elizabeth says, still sitting upright in bed. She combs her hair, taking one strand at a time.

I say nothing and the doctor does not reply. Instead, he says, "You're going to go with your mom. She needs to take you to University Hospitals where you'll have to stay for a couple of days."

Elizabeth's eyes widen. She doesn't know what's before her. I don't need to ask her how she feels. She'll give me her pat answer, "I'm getting away from you."

I don't want to be left alone with my daughter when she's in these moods, since she has lied to the authorities. I don't want to risk going through another child abuse investigation. The first time this happened, Elizabeth ran away in bare feet wearing a short skirt. Sun still heated the days, but autumn fingered the end of August at the time of night when most people give their last thoughts of the day to sleep. Two sheriff's deputies picked her up a couple of miles from our house. She told them that I had locked her out. Not true. She also told them that I had rubbed her nose in dog pee. True, I did.

One deputy didn't say a word when they brought her home. He hung back like a shadow. The other one said, "You got something to work out with your daughter?" Uniforms generate a feeling of inferiority in me, like I'm not tidy, not structured. He stood tall, omniscient-like and I had to raise my chin to see his face.

I walked a small circle. "Yes, we do, Sir." Thinking *if only you knew*. But I didn't know then what Elizabeth had told them I'd done to her. If I had known, I would have revealed our case.

After they left, I said, "Elizabeth, I worried about you. Where did you go? What happened?" I stood in the hallway by her bedroom, hoping she'd talk about what had transpired between us. "I'm sorry. I snapped. Nobody can take the constant yelling and screaming and demanding that you give to me."

"You locked me out of the house, so I was going to walk to a friend's house." She declared this loudly and sharply like the crack of a whip hitting a hard surface. She turned on me with beady eyes and a stiff posture.

"No! I didn't lock you out. I'd never do that!" My back ached and I stood with one hand on my forehead.

"YES, you did!" She shouted back, then slammed the door to her room.

I've heard that you'll never be the same if you see Coyote, that it's best not to go looking for her. Coyote turns your world upside down. Elizabeth turns my world upside down. Just when you think you've sorted things out and have direction, Coyote gets involved, playing games. Elizabeth twists my stomach, my emotions, my sanity.

My fiftieth birthday came two days later, the same day of the school board election forum. As a candidate, I had to sit on the panel. In retrospect, I wonder if my running for the board, giving and getting attention in the weeks that led up to the election, might have been the trigger that increased Elizabeth's anxieties, thereby culminating in the most recent rampage. But that day, I ran errands, drove to see friends, anything to keep myself busy, to not think about the evening's debate. In the afternoon, upon returning home, I found a note on my gate from an investigative social worker.

When the social worker paid me a visit, I opened up, let all spill out, telling him about the troubles we'd had with Elizabeth since the adoption, which were exacerbated by the accident. Afterward, the social worker drove to Elizabeth's school. There he talked to Elizabeth and to her teachers. After the social worker gathered information, he annulled the abuse allegation. More than that, he aided in Elizabeth's admission to a residential treatment school known for its guidance to foster and adoptive children. She lived there for six months.

Now that she has been referred to the university's psychiatric department, she may be headed to the same facility again.

Ruth, Elizabeth, and I sit in a claustrophobic waiting room down the hall from University Hospital's ER. What light we get comes from the hall. Straight chairs fit tightly side to side. We've checked in and the staff located Elizabeth's records from her visits as an outpatient in the child psychiatry department. The staff also received tonight's report from the other hospital. In fact, we've been here for a few hours and Mike will soon arrive to take Ruth home. It's already midnight.

Elizabeth continues to shift positions in her chair, leaning on me. I imagine sprawling out on my bed, having the cats cuddle up around me, listening to coyotes sing, sleeping until long after everyone in the world has gone to work. And then I conjure up an image of Coyote's den. It goes on in my head like an old song I can't stop singing because I've recently learned about wolves, how different they are from coyotes.

The wolf picks a life-long mate and forms a functioning family. With coyotes, the male stays with the female until the pups become teenagers. The male then leaves, and the young get the boot. With wolves, the family sticks together until the end and everyone has a job raising the pups. Taking this information into consideration, I'm a wolf. I believe in sticking together, helping each other out, confiding in each other. Adults need to love and nurture children. Children need to not worry about survival. Elizabeth, however, consistently prowls the territory, testing the alpha. She doesn't give up, nor does she walk away when I growl. Her violet irises turn black as she stands her ground and snarls.

When I finally leave the hospital and drive home, I continue to see Elizabeth as I left her, laying with her body toward the wall and her back to me after the nurses prepared her bed. "I love you, Elizabeth," I intimated. I had made a point to say that to both Raymond and Elizabeth at least once each day during my life with them, but in that particular moment, I wondered about the truth of my words. I put my hand on her shoulder and said, "I'll be back tomorrow."

She shrugged me away, "Don't bother."

At home, dried vomit sticks to everything in the hallway. The chair, the table, the walls, and the floor are covered with it. It reeks. I know I'll not sleep until the smell is gone so I get out the scrub brush and the bleach.

The clock reads 4:34 a.m. when I throw my clothes on top of the open suitcases. In the mirror, I see a huge bruise on my arm and I think to snap a photo of it. I'm learning how Elizabeth's mind works.

As I sleep, my dreams replay the circumstances that led up to my pushing her nose in Sasha's pee, the incident that led me to be investigated. Sasha has since died, but this moment still haunts me.

Elizabeth had wanted me to take her to the school dance. "If you don't, I'll kill you," she commanded. She faced me, hands on her hips, lips pursed, the black flecks in the deep blue of her irises stood out.

"It won't work that way, Elizabeth, and you know it. If you tend to your duties and ask nicely if you may go, you'll get to. We'll see on Friday how you've done for the week." I was cooking supper and I pushed the tone of her voice to the back of my mind; couldn't allow her to irritate me. Each day that week, and always, she vehemently refused to do chores. In fact, she refused to help with anything. She wouldn't even set the table.

"You want me to be your slave, and I won't!" She yelled, stomping her feet. She has said this consistently over the years. She never gives up telling herself she can't. I think *pity* to dampen my hostile reaction to her rages.

The day of the dance I told her she had another chance. I promised to help her with jobs if she would work on them. We completed the chores, and she began practicing her violin, which we'd agreed had to be done. I breathed a sigh of relief, thinking she'd get to go to the dance. But then, when only twelve minutes remained, she checked the time.

"You changed the timer!" One hand on her hip, with the other hand she shook the violin by its neck.

If I reminded her how to properly hold the violin, she'd surely choose to abuse it. No matter what way I turned, she'd goad me like a feral animal moving in for the kill. "No, I didn't, Elizabeth." Flabbergasted at her accusation, I turned toward her.

"You're a liar! I know you did! I refuse to practice anymore." She started swinging her violin by its tuning pegs.

"You've done so well! We can make this work. But acting like that isn't going to help your cause. Negotiate with me." My voice strained and it occurred to me that I wanted her to go to the dance more than she did.

"I don't care! You're a liar and I'm not going to do anything you say, and I *am* going to the dance and you will take me!"

I returned to cooking, saying, "If you stop now and finish practicing, you'll still have a chance to go." I set my lips, drew in my stomach and stretched my height.

Then she bellowed and threw the violin across the kitchen table. My stomach churned but I continued cooking, trying hard to focus on things outside the window. I watched the birds, watched the horses in the pasture, told myself not to react. *I can get through this.*

For more than an hour she threw books, papers, knickknacks, whatever she could grab. Then she threw her loaded backpack. It hit with a thump on my back, making me feel like I'd been heaved down onto jagged boulders. Seconds after the hit, I watched my husky, Sasha, who was ill with Cushing's disease, pee on the carpet. Elizabeth's screaming consistently triggered him to do this. I thought about how much I loved Sasha and how I wanted revenge for his sickness and for the discomfort that Elizabeth's conduct caused him.

The pee accounted for one more of so many messes that Elizabeth vehemently refused to clean up. I couldn't make her do it. If I told her she was grounded, she'd be pleased. When I took something away from her, her favorite skirt, for example, to discipline her, she didn't care. Nothing I did spoke to her. If I was nice to her, she spat in my face.

I looked at the mess. I looked at the backpack now on the floor and then at Elizabeth who continued screaming. "I hate you. You're a fucking bitch! Did you ever think there might be a reason why you didn't have your own kids?" She stood rigid in the kitchen doorway, her arms at her sides and her fists clenched.

Having sunk her teeth into my heart, she pounced to bring me down. Elizabeth has always assumed I couldn't bear children. I could have given birth but chose instead to give a child like her a family. Still, her insolence ripped through me like bared teeth. Screaming, yelling refusals, verbal abuse, and physical abuse. I'd been taking this for years from her, long before Raymond died.

I looked down at Sasha, who was looking up at me. His sick eyes begged for the peace and quiet that my own soul longed for. Elizabeth knew her yelling episodes upset him, but that never stopped her. Now, however, she did stop. Silence. Finally. A strange calm began to overtake me. Coyote yips wafted through the open window. The sun had stepped aside for the oncoming hours. Frustration rolled in with the changing barometer. No time for self-restraint, nor for second-guessing. I grabbed the back of Elizabeth's neck, forced her to bend down, and shoved her nose into the pee. "See what you do to the animals! You don't give a damn about anybody but yourself!" Then, I let go of her and began to cry, wishing with all my heart that Raymond had lived.

In my recurring dream after I return home from University Hospitals, I see myself push Elizabeth down into the pee. Then I awake. Shortly, I go back into a sleep where I dream the same haunting scene over and over.

Coyotes travel alone unless small prey become scarce. Then a group may gang up on a larger vulnerable animal, one lacking in strength. Coyotes have been known to bring down an older, lone wolf, but if a coyote poaches on wolf territory, the wolves have no mercy.

Elizabeth and I, of different species, share the same den. Scared and vulnerable, both hungry for solace. She needed me to withstand the rage inside of her, to bear the attacks and snarls, and yet enjoy the few songs to balance the terrified, caged pup inside of her. I wanted to assuage her wounds, but I had my own constitution twirling from one mood to the next. I couldn't settle in my own heart. I listened to social workers, to teachers, and to therapists, hoping they had answers to mend Elizabeth's mental torment. Yet their advice befuddled me. Each counsel stemmed from the repertoire of redundant, normal circumstances and ordinary families with average children. To explain Elizabeth's and my situation took stamina that no longer existed in me. To myself, I surrendered as unfit to parent.

Images of broken opportunities to reach out and comfort Elizabeth plagued me. After the accident, when I remained strapped to my bed to prevent me from moving, the hospital released Elizabeth to Mary, my sister, for care. Upon my discharge, Mary and her daughter, Molly, took me in, too. I recall overwhelming pain throughout those days. Pain filled my mind, too, but one afternoon I awoke in a chair to find Elizabeth standing over me, just watching. Small and thin, her face drawn, and her pupils enlarged, revealing her defenseless and fragile composition.

"This is hard for you, Elizabeth," I said, searching for more words, more thoughts, but none came. She didn't respond. I wanted to hug her, but given the injuries I had, I couldn't physically do that. I could barely move. She turned around and walked away.

Perhaps, if I'd been able to hug her, if she'd felt the embodiment of love in that moment, the next few years would have been easier.

When I visit Elizabeth in the psychiatric ward, she tells me that she doesn't want to go home, that she wants a new family. We sit on couches where the professionals can observe us. I'm of two minds about her being here. On one hand, I'm relieved to have time to myself, to finally have quiet. On the other, I cry a lot. I want her to smile, to be asked to dances by nice boys, to receive awards at school for achievements, and to go to games with friends. I want her to come home from school and tell me about her day, not pummel me with hatred.

Still, I cry a lot anyway, missing my pups. One, Raymond passed away. The other, Elizabeth, turned into an uncivilized organism. Her natural environment invaded by grief and suffering, those merciless poachers that have crazed her mind.

"You don't think of me as your mom," I say this as matter-of-factly as possible, even though I can hear the accusatory tone in it. Her statement about wanting a new family hurts as much as the thrown backpack did.

"But I do!" She turns her head toward me, and I see the dark circles under her eyes. This darkness has stayed with her through the years. Sleep never came easy for her.

At home, I look in the mirror. Darkness spreads around my eyes, too. How could it not? My frequent crying over Elizabeth's internal agony and praying for her life to even out keeps me awake nights, too.

Elizabeth's psychiatrist at the university tells me my weepiness and being on edge is a result of the concussion and the brain trauma. Healing may take months, maybe years, she tells me. Understanding that my fears and my tears are organic rather than self-imposed helps me to let down my guard. I stop trying to hide the fact that my mind doesn't work as it once did, or as I think it should.

Elizabeth's discharge orders take her to a group home for at-risk teenagers until she gains readmission to the residential treatment school she attended before. In the group home, one young worker tells Elizabeth the plan, that she awaits a vacancy. Hoping to prevent going there and desiring a foster home placement instead, Elizabeth shows the worker her back. She calls it a bruise and says that I did that to her. She has always had an area of darkened skin on her back, but the young worker falls for it and files an abuse report.

A few days later, the same investigative social worker, who visited me after the sheriff deputies picked Elizabeth up on the road, comes to see me again. I show him my arm, the bruise yellowing with age. Although the reason of his visit wracks my nerves, I do enjoy our conversation. Again, he proves to be understanding and helpful and speeds up the process for Elizabeth's re-admittance. Her trick has failed her. She has stepped into her own trap, naively and unknowingly set by her own doing.

I walk the social worker to his car and wave goodbye. As I return to the house, I see Coyote's scat again. She's alone, like me, her family split up and gone.

Coyote's nature pushes her to strike out on her own but before she does, Mother Coyote teaches her survival skills. I haven't been able to teach Elizabeth these skills. Instead, in her quest for independence she developed her own. Her freedom comes with a formidable price of falling into an underworld, into a den of mental illness that clouds her judgment.

Does the mother coyote worry when pushing her pup out into the cruel world? Does she think about all the things that could happen? Does she realize that the orneriest one may be the one least prepared to take care of itself?

With Elizabeth settled into her new temporary life, I groom the horse each day, spend more time working with the dogs, reading, and writing. I pump up my physical therapy prescribed by my doctor after the accident to several times a week to condition for my own dogsled trip. A more rigorous expedition than the one I had planned with Elizabeth. I'll be camping out on a frozen lake, hearing wolves in the distance, and conducting the dogs that transport the sled.

Every tenth day, I drive a four-hour round trip to attend counseling sessions with Elizabeth. Five months have passed since a friend helped me transport Elizabeth from the youth home to the treatment school. The treatment is going well, and I am both hopeful and suspicious of the improvements I see in her.

At present, I am sitting in a stuffed chair across from her and her counselor. No darkness gathers around Elizabeth's eyes. She wears a ponytail neatly combed back. Her jeans and t-shirt appear freshly washed.

"Do you have questions for your daughter?" Shawn, the therapist, says, "Ask her anything you need to."

I like this counselor. She doesn't ruffle, and she doesn't miss a beat, either. When Elizabeth tells a story differently, Shawn calls her on it, throwing out thoughts that make Elizabeth accountable without accusing either of us.

Sitting there, many questions tumble through my mind. So much needs to be asked and so much needs to be remedied. "What, Elizabeth, made you so mean to the animals?" I ask her. I'm thinking of the time Elizabeth kicked our pup, Ella. Her foot hit square in the ribs and when Ella yelped, rolled over, Elizabeth stomped toward her as though she'd smash right into her. Fortunately, Ella could get up and she ran.

Kimo, Raymond's cat, the cat that forever purrs and rubs, who loves to sit on laps for hours, stood in Elizabeth's path one day. She grabbed his tail and pulled hard. Another time when it was her job to give the horses water, she let them go thirsty when it was beastly hot. That day, I filled the tub with water myself and the horses slurped it up faster than I could put it in the trough. More recently, Elizabeth's screams have made Ella tremble and hide behind the sofa, and when Sasha hears her, he pees on the carpet. Elizabeth sees them react to her, terrified, but she doesn't stop. Instead, she brings the yowls from deeper in her diaphragm, louder, and longer.

Here, in the therapist's room, I continue, "I understand your animosity toward me, but not them." My eyes moisten. My hands hold tight to the arms of the chair. My arm muscles tense. I am not sure I'm ready for her answer, but I must know it. Maybe this child will always be an abuser. Maybe the early crimes committed against her define her character, and she has no capability to reform. Perhaps, her recent improvements are just temporary.

Elizabeth looks at Shawn who nods back at her. Then Elizabeth shifts her position on the couch. We sit a coffee table apart from each other. She leans forward, knees pressed together. She looks me in the eye, her pupils wide. Somewhere down in there I detect a soul. "You loved the animals and neglecting them got to you," she says. "Now, I feel awful that I did those things." She hesitates, as both Shawn and I listen. "But everything I did was to make myself hate you, and to keep you from loving me. I've had too many losses. I didn't want to be close to you because I might lose you, too." Her eyes are moist. She sits tall and leans back into her chair. Her legs ease to the side of the couch.

Can I believe this? Could she make that up, thinking that's what I want to hear? I ask her.

"No," she says. "No." She continues to look at me.

I am convinced for now. I smile and tears roll down my cheeks. I sigh. Elizabeth smiles, a tender and true smile, too.

Wolf Mom slaps her big paw on the pup when it misbehaves, licks it all over when it runs to her. I hug Elizabeth before I leave for home this day. She hugs me back. We are standing by my car. We're alone together.

We're not running free yet. I understand the battle to cure Elizabeth of RAD doesn't end so easily. At Shawn's recommendation, Elizabeth will finish out high school at a boarding school, though during her vacations she will live with me. Peer therapy has helped Elizabeth to see that her contrary attitude isn't benefiting her. So, the treatment center staff advises that living with peers, instead of living as an only child, will aid her emotional development. At home, Elizabeth and I will tangle, and we will also have soul-searching talks. But she can finally express her emotions verbally and rationally. This is a new beginning for both of us, especially for her.

I turn onto the gravel road that leads to our home. Twilight covers the countryside. In my peripheral vision, I see a figure run alongside my car then dash in front of it. Coyote. I slow down, open the car windows. From the pastures all around me, coyotes are chanting.

CHAPTER
Seven

SHE RODE

I n my late teens, my father insisted upon selling my horses. Off to college, I had left them in his care, and he no longer wanted the responsibility. Two of my three had been sold to people who would treat them well. Regrettably, I sold my big mare, Margo, to a neighbor. When I was ten, riding past his place, I had jumped off my pony and run to this same man, had grabbed the whip from his hand and pleaded with him to stop using it on the brown and white horse who pulled back hard on the lead, its eyes white with terror.

Eleven years after that incident, my mom and I sat in my parent's living room. Mom's neck projected out from her humped and deformed spine. She had been diagnosed with osteoporosis and breast cancer in a time when doctors knew not much about either. She had surgery for a radical mastectomy and some of her vertebrae had crumbled. "You had spunk as a little one," Mom said, and recounted the time that old man came to our farm to complain about me taking his whip away.

"I didn't want my horse to go to that man," I told her.

Mom urged me to visit Margo, and so that afternoon I did. When I drove into the old man's farm, he stood in the yard. He stared at me as I climbed out of my car, then he nodded toward the cattle.

"She won't let ya get near. She's wild." I didn't acknowledge what he said, walked past him and opened the rusted-steel cattle gate enough to slip by. I wore dress pants and a silk blouse with the Irish-tweed jacket I had made. My new black boots picked up mud and hog and cattle muck from the spring thaw.

I made my way through the yard, aiming for the big chestnut mare with the cream mane and tail, the only horse amongst all the cattle. Her head held high, she watched me and as I got closer, she lowered her head, walked toward me. We met. She put her head on my chest. I put my hands on her face, around her eyes and whispered, "I'm sorry that you can't be with me anymore." I drew in her sweet smell, took a minute to stroke her neck and then turned away, my cheeks wet. She followed me for a few steps, then stopped.

I passed by the man on the way to my car. I saw the hardness in his face, the swollen cheeks, the wrinkles, and the smell of seldom-laundered clothes. I wanted to buy back the mare as much as I wanted my mother to live. Unfortunately, I had no control over either. As I drove away from that man's farm, my eyes felt heavy and sore, same as my mood. My mare's sweet scent, swishing tail and head on my shoulder lingered in my senses.

Since then, I have strayed far from my youthful dream of raising horses, but I have never stopped longing for another one.

When my husband Jon and I bought eight acres, I immediately began reading newspaper ads, looking online, and checking with people who had horses. By the time my children, Elizabeth age twelve, and Raymond age eleven, and I checked out Max for the second time, I had looked at thirteen horses and gone to two sale barns. I wanted a bombproof horse, one that nothing could frighten, one that could be trusted with children, and yet big enough for me to ride. Max stood about fourteen hands. Perfect. His blue-roan coloring and black mane and tail gave him a look of nobility. He stood quietly; his ears erect. While Elizabeth mounted him, he walked carefully around the yard, making her feel at ease. She slid off and I put my foot in the stirrup, and with my hand on the saddle horn, pulled up and swung on.

Leaning over, I grabbed Raymond's arm and he jumped up behind me. Max didn't flinch any more than if a fly had landed on his back.

"Will you take any less?" I asked the man selling him. I expected "no" for an answer. The man raised and trained registered quarter horses. With limited funds, though, I had to think about feed and building fences, and all else that comes with owning a horse.

"I know what I've got..." He said, turning to Max, a look of reluctance on his face.

And before he could finish, I said, "I'll take him." I wrote out a check and we made arrangements for him to deliver Max.

Driving home, I fought with myself. I worried about spending the money, about how Jon would react to this purchase. He knew I had been looking at horses, but he would not join in, nor discuss the possibility of owning a horse. In another time, I would have thought out such a purchase with deliberation. I would have insisted that Jon discuss it with me. But some internal force drove me to acquire Max now. An overwhelming sensation that something loomed, that time charged ahead, and goaded me to cram everything possible into each day. Despite this, through the rear-view mirror, I grinned at Raymond and Elizabeth in the back seat. "You're going to love this horse!" I said, one hand slapping the steering wheel with glee.

Before the children and I left to see Max this time, I had told Jon I would probably buy this horse. Back home, I informed Jon I'd written the check. We had no defined pasture, nor did we have a shelter. Winter brewed in Iowa; north winds blew cold and night temperatures stood below freezing. Jon said nothing. His face had an illegible look. His eyes didn't change and his mouth neither smiled nor frowned. In all the years I'd talked about getting a horse, he hadn't expressed any aversion to it. But then he hadn't supported the idea, either. He had advocated for Elizabeth to go to horse camp each summer. But now, not knowing exactly what Jon thought, I suddenly felt as though I'd done the wrong thing. The joy I'd imagined experiencing with this purchase turned into anxiety.

As a child, I had developed physical and mental skills working with horses, and they had been great companions for me. I wanted to pass this on to my children. And, though my own mother hadn't taken a great interest in my horses, she had appreciated my admiration and ability to work with them. She had supported me. I could see that both of my children had an inclination to learn about horses and to learn to ride. I wanted to offer them a life of participating in shows and trail rides, events my dad hadn't allowed me to do. I had ridden my horses for transportation to 4-H meetings and for my own pleasure.

So, I had selfish reasons for buying Max—nostalgia and for my own enjoyment. I was struggling to be a good mom. I couldn't turn to my own mother for advice on my marriage, or raising my children, but I could relive the days when she lived, when insouciance defined my life. In the back of my mind, a horse symbolized just that. Yet, Jon's impassivity about the horse, and many other things, unnerved me. I felt disapproval and it spoke louder than if he'd verbally condemned me. I had grown tired of his negativity and my sensitivity heightened with his undefined mood.

On the Saturday morning of Max's scheduled transport, Jon still had not responded to my request for fencing materials. I began making calls to have tubular corral fencing brought in when I saw Jon leave in his pickup. A couple of hours later he returned with fencing, plywood, and studs in the truck bed. I went outside to help unload the materials and to thank him. Never a person to say, "You're welcome," or "It's nothing," he just didn't answer me.

The next morning, I heard Jon yelling at the children, who ran through the pasture, giggling and leaping and dancing together. Jon had expected their help with constructing the fence and a small shelter. Elizabeth and Raymond, however, had other ideas about readying for the newest addition to the family.

When the horse trailer drove into the yard, all four of us hurried from the house. I said the dogs, Sasha and Jack, should be left in the house. We needed to introduce them to Max carefully. Though Max had lived with dogs, he didn't know these, and Sasha and Jack had never been around a horse. Elizabeth and Raymond honored that, but Jon, last out, let the dogs out.

Max backed out of the trailer and both dogs began barking and running around him. It didn't rile Max, but with my nerves on edge, I worried chaos might ensue. Then, for no apparent reason, Raymond began crying and ran to the back porch. Elizabeth stood staring at Max from several feet away. Jon did the same, not offering any greeting to the man and his wife who had brought Max. The man said, "You've not got any fences."

Jon said, "I had no idea we were getting a horse."

Shocked that he'd say that, I said, "Yeah, Jon never knows what I might do." And I laughed, trying to make Jon's comment sound like a joke. With that, I went after Raymond.

"Ray, why are you crying?" I put my hands on his shoulders and he turned away from me, then he shuffled his thin, athletic body close to the wall.

"Because Max is for Elizabeth, and she gets everything. I want a horse."

"Max is for all of us, Ray. Whoever grooms him and feeds him and spends time with him will be the one that he chooses."

"Really?" He said, wiping the tears off his face.

"Yup. Come take Max's lead and I'll get the dogs in."

By the time I shook hands and said goodbye to the man and woman, Jon had a reel of electric fencing in his hand and Elizabeth carried some plastic posts.

In the rush of work, school, soccer games, violin and piano lessons, and Max, Jon's birthday flew by. I forgot to make a cake but the children picked out a card. "When life settles down," I promised him, "I'll make it up to you." I continued to attempt to make things right, although we never did celebrate that birthday. If Jon did care that his birthday had been skipped, he didn't say so. He rarely commented about anything, actually. He lived in his own world and not in the one in which the rest of us partook. He behaved unsociably in other situations, too, even in his work environment. By this time, our fifteenth year of marriage, I often wondered why I continued to try to smooth out the wrinkles that he created. Life with him exhausted me.

Each morning after the family left, before I began work, I put a halter and lead rope on Max and stood him to graze in the yard. I patted his neck, ran my hands along his back, down his legs. I lifted his hooves. He continued pulling at the grass, his teeth ripping the strands shortened and browned by the season. Sometimes he lifted his head and bumped me gently with his nose. Jack ran around him barking his jealousy. My other dog, Sasha, ill and old before his time, lingered close in, needing to be near me.

As the sunlight paled in the late afternoons, I saddled Max and rode him, then waited by the gate for Elizabeth and Raymond. When the school bus stopped, they raced down the steps, bumping each other this way and that, the bottoms of their shoes kicking up and down on the gravel in their rush to leave their books and coats in the house, to race back outside and ride. Elizabeth, having gone to riding camp in the summers, knew how to rein a horse.

Ray had no fears. He would calmly sit on Max, saddled or not. "Teach me how to ride, Mom. Please, please teach me how to ride!"

I intended for Raymond to take professional lessons when warm weather surfaced. Meanwhile, the days became colder, buckets of water quickly iced over. Each morning and night, one of us would carry five gallons of warm water and dump it in Max's fifteen-gallon plastic tub.

One day as I lugged a bucket of water to the pasture, Jack, already there, circled Max, barking. Max spun, keeping his head toward Jack until Sash wandered beyond the fence. Max trotted toward Sasha and kicked him. I dropped the bucket, spilling the water, and ran to Sasha, swooped him up in my arms and took him to the house. I had witnessed in Max's first home, his benevolent behavior with dogs. I surmised that here, Max sensed a lack of knowledge about his kind. Jon had no experience with horses and some time had passed since I had worked with equines. Admittedly, I felt hesitant about Max's needs and that doubt could have been enough to cause Max to test his position.

Another day, Max bit me hard on my forearm, forming a blood bruise. I smacked his nose. He drew back, eyes wide. I knew that slapping him could make him head shy, but I felt agitated. An undercurrent of trouble brewed inside me. Always preoccupied, even when around the animals, I obsessed about the children, especially Elizabeth, who often had behavior troubles at school, which, in turn, may have caused her learning problems. At home, she refused to help with anything. She yelled and screamed at homework time and increasingly talked Raymond into running away with her to the river. Raymond experienced difficulties at school, as well, though not to the same degree. Jon, plagued by the library board that wanted to oust him, took his frustrations out at home. He refused to back up disciplines that I set for Elizabeth, though he would not set any of his own. Elizabeth taunted Raymond, called him nasty names in front of other students and dared him to run away several times. Some nights, Raymond would confide in me, weeping about Elizabeth's betrayal. When I tried to talk to her about behavior, she'd yell, slam doors, and let loose the loud force of her lungs. When I would ask Jon to work in accordance with me, he usually said nothing, nor promised anything.

Whatever Raymond did or said Jon often criticized, sometimes flicking his fingers on Raymond's head for no apparent reason. Raymond had a great sense of humor, but he took certain things, such as piano lessons, seriously. He definitely had an innate musical gift. Jon, unfortunately, rarely acknowledged Raymond's accomplishments.

Though Max didn't try to bite again, his show of orneriness happened more frequently. He must have perceived my distress and perplexity, as horses have such sensitivity. Similar incidents within the family transpired and weight entered my breath. Arising in the mornings became a task. The feeling of being rushed, of our lives spinning out of control, pressed in. The animals felt it. Sasha clung to me and Jack barked out of control. Max laid back his ears often, stamped his hooves. My mother, dead now for twenty-nine years, began to frequent my memories.

In the days when my mother's health escaped her, pain kept her bedridden. Her eyes held a glassy look to them. She didn't want to eat. An atmosphere of malaise, a scarcity of Mom's presence encompassed our small farmhouse. She no longer could bring in vegetables from the garden, nor go to the basement freezer for a chunk of meat to cook. I moved home to help. The laundry, left to my doing, went from the washer to the dryer. I wouldn't take the time to spread it over the line to bring in the outdoors-clean scent, as she had done throughout my youth. The den had been made into her bedroom. Dad and I hovered about, ready to retrieve whatever Mom might request.

One afternoon, she wanted to sit up. I helped her put on the pink robe that I had made for her and guided her to a chair near the bed. She gasped for breath until the air moved more easily in and out of her lungs. Then she spoke, "No one else in the family will listen to me about dying. So, you must." My forehead ached and I covered my eyes, certain that they would pop out of my head from sadness. My throat closed and I couldn't answer her.

"Say the Prayer to Our Lady every day and you'll have what you need. Remember, she is Mother, and she will guide you."

Mom advised other things, too, but her urgency frightened me. An internal nagging commenced. Not so much that I heard it with my ears, rather it compelled my psyche. I washed windows, meticulously checked for streaks, ran dust rags over the furniture and knickknacks, carefully ensured that no particles remained. Then I vacuumed the rugs, pushing and pulling the sweeper. I became obsessed with just doing something instead of sitting still.

Elizabeth and Raymond had ridden in the back seat on the day I drove to write a check for Max, leaving the front passenger seat vacant. As I steadied the van's wheel on a gravel road, a sudden, unmistakable scent of Chantilly perfume wafted beneath my nose. I had not perceived that fragrance, my mother's favorite, since before she died. As quickly as I sniffed it, it disappeared. Puzzled by this, I decided she had appeared to me, the only explanation I could fathom. Had she come to offer me comfort? Or had she come to caution me? Whatever the intent, it reminded me of the looming feeling of doom I had had before her death—that same oppression I had been feeling in the passing weeks.

***

Two months following Max's arrival at our place, Jon and Raymond died in the collision with the semi. I had multiple life-threatening injuries. Though Elizabeth escaped physical injury, the accident left her psychologically devastated.

Doctors and family allowed me to return home after twenty days. Elizabeth, who had stayed with my sister, Mary, joined me. Friends and family took turns staying with us, tending to the animals, washing the laundry, and fixing meals. Each day, I walked a quarter mile on the gravel road. My legs felt like giant tree stumps. My torso, neck, and head constricted into pain, a burning home of flames leaping from the basement to the attic. My mind functioned like swirling air; thoughts flew by, but none held. I remained corpse-like, flat on my back, loaded with ibuprofen and codeine to assuage the physical misery.

No one told me, and if they did, it had not registered, that head injuries plus emotional trauma make a person incapable of good judgment. I couldn't assess Elizabeth's, nor my needs. When people asked if we needed continual live-in help, I declined, terrified of becoming a nuisance. So, we continued muddling our way through. Elizabeth managed to get on the school bus each morning. I dragged myself from bed, walked to the door in time to wave goodbye to her, and crawled back under the covers.

One Saturday morning, I heard a strange noise coming from below my room. Max stood on the back porch looking in the house. He had torn the sliding glass door screens, slicing them into hanging wires. Elizabeth lured him back to the pasture with a bucket of food. But the next day, he stepped through the fence again. This happened many times, over several days, until I called a neighbor whose land bordered mine. In a cranky mood, he repaired the fence but treated me as an annoying idiot. Because I could walk, and I appeared functional, he must have thought I merely wanted attention. His fence repair didn't hold, though.

In a heavy snowstorm, Max escaped again. This time, he hung out by the front door. Elizabeth rushed to get the pail of oats. I took the halter from its hook in the laundry room. Max, lonely, put his nose in my hand. In reaching up to slip the halter over his ears, my back and ribs flared with stabbing spasms. I stood still, waiting for breath to come easier. Snow built on Max's back and face. When finally I forced myself to walk, I expected Max to follow. He balked.

Elizabeth screamed, "You screwed up everything! He would have followed me!" Her yelling caused Max to rear up. I turned toward him to pull down on the lead and his front hoof struck my thighs. In the deep snow, I stumbled, falling to my knees. Max's great body lingered above me. Then, snorting, he ran, the spate of snow from his hooves landing on me.

I craved to be the horsewoman I had once been. But I had no influence. No strength left in my weary body. In that moment when I could not take charge, horse and girl had demoted me. And so, I stayed in the billowing snow, rolled up in a fetal position.

Long ago, I had lain down in similar conditions. Was I fourteen? Fatigued from mononucleosis, I had slept in an open pasture, untroubled by the falling white fluff until my mother found me and walked me home where she piled blankets on me. She made me tea and brought me soup.

Where did she go when she died? Now, an impossible wish overwhelmed me. I wanted my mother to return and fix this mess of my life. The mere thought of her brought me comfort. She would help me up, take me away from the blizzard that pelted my face, from the throbbing in my legs that I knew without even looking had quickly turned to contusions. I grasped this notion of Mom's return, prayed to make it truth, knowing the impossibilities.

Tempted to remain curled up, disregarding responsibilities, I thought of Elizabeth. She strained for control in her life. Distraught at having lost her birth family, her anger now boiled due to the deaths of her little brother and adoptive father. She needed comfort and guidance. I had been handed this task. My mother would have known how to handle Elizabeth's behavior. I did not know what to do with her relentless screaming, her kicking me, her running away, her refusal to do her homework and to participate in school activities. Consistently, purposefully, she broke things. She busted the neck on her violin, threw dishes on the floor, smashed small statues in her room.

I looked at my hands, red from cold, felt my stiffening face. Snow covered my hair and my eyelashes. I felt its wetness, felt the wind blast, heard it howling. I came to my knees, slowly getting up. Elizabeth had already retreated to the house where I gradually walked. Grateful that the melting snow dripping down my face disguised the accompanying salty stream.

In my room, from where I lay on the bed, I looked at the display on my oak secretary. Over the years, each time I moved to a new home, I set up the statue of the Blessed Mary that I had won in second-grade catechism class for reciting Mother Mary's prayer without fault. Statues of horses surrounded the icon, which, until then, had been a subconscious placement. As I looked at the images, it occurred to me that the loss of my mother and of my horses connected directly with my feelings to the loss of Jon and Raymond. I had felt defeated all those years without horses. When my mother died, I, being the youngest by far of all the siblings, and despite my father still living, I felt orphaned. All my siblings had begun their own lives with their own families. Earnestly, I had tried to make a family with Jon and Raymond and had attempted a motherly bond with Elizabeth.

Lying on my side, I looked at the oak piece, the same books, the same mementos from decades before, things that had always comforted me. My thoughts traveled back in time.

The day before Mom's death, I felt its imminence. I could not find the courage to speak to my father about what transpired before us. I'm sure he didn't want to face the truth, either. Instead of staying home with my mother, I drove to two of her sisters' homes. And, then I went to my paternal sister's abode. Aunts all of whom I loved. None of these visits had been planned. I had no known reason for going from one to the others all in the same day. Scared and so young, I felt desperate. I silently pleaded for help, hoped to find solace in the company of my aunts.

Finding Aunt Bub, my mother's youngest sister, in the kitchen fixing lunch, I cried out. "I don't think Mom's going to live much longer!"

My aunt hugged me. "Let me fix you a sandwich. You need lunch." She ignored my words.

I refused to sit down with her. "I must go. I have errands I need to do. I'm really not hungry anyway."

I drove next to an older sister of mom's, Aunt Leone. I sat in her over-stuffed chair, and we talked of novels. My fingers ran up and down the chair arm. Occasionally, I rubbed my legs, smoothing out my pants from my lap to my knees. Aunt Leone seemed fidgety, too, pressing the fingers of each hand against the other. After a while she said, "You seem distracted?"

"I think Mom is dying!" I choked out. "I need to go."

Aunt Leone wrapped her hand in mine and led me down the front hall in silence. Before I opened the door to leave, she gently squeezed my hand.

Next, I drove to Aunt Marieta's apartment. We exchanged pleasantries. Immediately then, I blurted out, "I think Mom is dying!"

"Oh! Don't say that. Your mom won't die!" She asked me to sit down, to have some tea, or a soda.

But, I said, "No! No! I have to go home."

As I stopped to tell each aunt that Mom's death grew near, I became overwhelmed with sorrow. On the run from my emotions, I assured myself the company of my aunts would replace the impending loss with something I could hold onto. But as I stopped at each house, I realized nothing would erase the void. Nothing would ever be able to replace Mom's absence. Clearly, I faced the dead end of denial.

The episode in the snow with Max and Elizabeth had fatigued me. During my own convalescence, every activity wore me out. Recalling the days before Mom's death slipped me into deep sleep. When I awoke, the house neared darkness. I could hear Elizabeth playing a radio in her room. Outside, the snowstorm carried on. I remained on my back, contemplating the day's events.

Herd animals like horses need companionship and a leader. Max had not been with us long enough to feel secure when the accident happened. Then, having been left alone except for feedings, he discerned the turmoil. Like Elizabeth, who had barely turned thirteen, Max, a young horse, needed guidance.

Elizabeth could not take responsibility for Max. She could barely function in her own world of school and friends. Certain things, like working with horses at summer camps, had helped her gain some confidence, but her character, formed by abuses and neglect in her early years, remained anxiety-ridden. Any ground gained toward healing in the seven years within our family, she seemed to have lost in the accident. Now she feared all sorts of situations: working with Max; riding in a car; playing her violin; and what her peers might or might not say. In a word, she rejected most everything, but it came across as recurrent anger, directed toward anything in her world. I could not trust her to stay alone. I never knew what she might do, or if she might be self-destructive.

The first year after the auto accident, my neurological abilities had been tested. Written results stated, "reason for concern." The second year, upon testing, my cognitive function recorded within normal range for duties involving simple cognition. The doctors gave me an okay to hold a "mindless"—my word, not theirs—job. My boss, after the accident, had held my position open for eight months, providing me an open opportunity to return. I had tried two times to take over where I left off, but when I would speak to adoptive parents, I would begin to cry uncontrollably. Now I didn't seek employment because I had Elizabeth to look out for. Having suffered the trauma of a concussion and multiple head injuries, my mind didn't function in the way it once had. I didn't know how to deal with my new thought processes. I couldn't even define it.

Over and above that, I'd taken on single parenting to a troubled teenager. Consequently, unexpected difficulties developed. I didn't really know how to talk to Elizabeth and her frequent screaming triggered my own anger. Ordinary day-to-day needs, simple as cooking supper, became challenges. I worried that if I confided in others that my mind did not work correctly, something would be taken from me, Elizabeth maybe, or the animals. Or would I be put in some sterile place and become a drug experiment? These paranoid thoughts accompanied me, yet outwardly I managed to work with my attorney regarding the accident. I also kept Elizabeth fed and in school, cared for the animals, and paid the bills.

Then one day my doctor said, "Your lung and ribs and vertebrae should be healed. Continue with physical therapy and be careful not to overdo." And though my body mended, pain remained as a constant reminder of being thrust into the unknown. My soul ached as much as any other part, too. Anticipating that working with Max would restore what had gone amiss in my spirit, I began to spend time with him. He liked to be busy and liked to play. He'd grab the zipper tab on my jacket with his lips and pull it up and down. Occasionally though, he'd bite, which I took as a reminder of my unrelenting fragility.

Despite both Elizabeth's and my troubles, I wanted her to ride him believing that it would grant her some peace. In my confused state, I had no sense about the possible danger to Elizabeth, a novice horse rider. She lacked the skills to guide a troubled horse. Her anger only provoked the unrest in Max. When she approached him, he moved about, restlessly snorting and stomping his feet. However she may have read this behavior, it prompted her to play a game with him. In the pasture, she chased him. In return, he chased her. I watched through the window. Their give-and-take stirred up the snow so that a whirlwind hid them.

"The game you play isn't a good discipline for Max," I said to Elizabeth. "And it could be dangerous for you. If you slipped and fell while he ran at you..." Out of spite, then, and any time when she knew I watched, especially when others visited us, she lured Max into the game.

Yet, I continued to hope that Max could soothe Elizabeth's injured soul. I believed that her healing would emerge through a relationship with Max, and when that happened, she would be as I had been at her age; she could seek emotional refuge in this horse. My own injured psyche, and the pain of all my losses would be mitigated through Elizabeth's experience.

I continued to witness my daughter's broken spirit and I talked to others about her behavior and her sadness. The talk, also a release for me, allowed me to gain ideas that hadn't occurred to me.

One day, I told Amy, a neighbor who owned, trained, and showed American Quarter horses, about Max and Elizabeth's behaviors. Amy told me about an elderly mare, a retired barrel racer, a calm horse that needed a home. If sold, the mare would probably end up in the slaughterhouse. If I took her, she might be the key to helping Elizabeth conquer her apprehensions. A companion for Max might possibly resolve his negative conduct.

Elizabeth and I spotted Pretty Sassy Girl from the road. She stood aloof from the herd. A sorrel, she had two white socks and a blaze down her forehead. Though she had a swayed back, she had the head of a young colt. She reminded me of a filly born outside my bedroom window when I was thirteen. Better yet, Elizabeth liked her. Sassy did have heaves, a condition akin to human asthma. Her hay and dry food needed to be moistened to relieve the symptoms, but that didn't deter us. We promised to take good care of her.

When Sassy strode into our pasture, she touched noses with Max. From then on, they walked side by side. When he attempted to confiscate Sassy's food, she gave him a disgruntled whinny, turned her backside to him and bucked. With us, Max continued to rear when haltered, as he had done with me in the snowstorm, refusing to cooperate. That summer, Amy and her daughter, Tessa, volunteered to move Max to their place and work with him. Elizabeth and I visited several times a week, usually finding Max tethered to a tree as a reprimand for rearing or biting.

"You know that if a horse rears high enough and falls backwards, he can be maimed, or killed," Amy said to me.

I nodded. Tempted to pat his neck instead of gazing at him from several feet away, I refrained because his rehabilitation required not

spoiling him. Max's behavioral treatment reminded me of what therapists had advised for Elizabeth, to ignore her nasty behavior and not
give her attention.

"He needs to go to a trainer who has that expertise of taking him
over backwards without hurting him. The only thing that can break a
horse of that rearing up is falling over backwards, which scares them.
But, in doing that, he could break a leg, or his back, anything. Still,
until he learns not to rear, he's dangerous."

I nodded and sighed. "Let's do it."

The next day, Amy called me. As Tessa had led Max from the
pasture to prepare him for his trip to a new trainer, he protested. He
asserted his power by rearing up so high that he took himself all the
way over.

"He's fine," Amy assured me. "It scared us, though."

"And Tessa?" I fretted, pacing the hallway, phone in hand.

"She wasn't riding him. Of course, she's good."

After I pushed the off button on the telephone, I sat on the front
porch and watched Sassy graze out in the pasture. I felt my jaw relax. I
hadn't known that I'd been grinding my teeth while thinking about
what might have happened to Max during the retraining. Now, given
that he'd learned his lesson, Elizabeth and I could begin working with
him again.

On evenings when Amy and Tessa rode their horses, I worked with
Max in their arena. Before being saddled to ride, he needed to be
longed, an exercise routine that settled his frisky edge. To longe a
horse, a long rope, maybe twenty feet, is clipped to its halter. The
handler positions herself in a direct line behind the animal's shoulder.
Ideally, the person stays in one place and slowly turns as the horse
walks, trots, or canters in a circle on a relaxed length of the rope. Max,
however, often pulled to the outside, tightening the rope between us,
jerking me from where I stood in the middle of the ring. Keeping him
on a steady course caused the recurrence of shooting pains in my back
and ribs. It wore me down.

Eight months had passed since the accident and I still continued
with physical therapy. My doctor had advised me not to ride, exactly

what I did not want to hear. I feared that my limitations, both physical and mental, might be permanent.

Since my childhood, directing horses, moving and being with them, fulfilled me. The creak of the leather, the sweet aroma, the warmth of the muscular body, connected me to the animal's intangible essence. Beholding such duality as the giving of the horse's self, yet retaining his freeness, rooted me. It defined the moment, sending waves of joy into my soul. Besides writing, it's the only thing I ever truly loved doing.

One evening, Elizabeth brought Max in from Amy's pasture and led him to the arena. He followed her lead easily without pulling or rushing ahead. Though I felt more comfortable engaging Max when Amy and Tessa rode close by, I prepared to longe him.

"Give me the rope," Elizabeth demanded.

I handed the line to her while Max trotted around us. "Keep behind his shoulder, Elizabeth, that's what motivates him to move forward." I stepped back a bit as I said this to show her.

"You think you know about horses but you don't know anything!" She shouted and dropped the rope on the ground. I picked it up, holding my patience. Elizabeth's defiance toward guidance and her loud voice exasperated me. In spite of this, we worked Max together. On this night, as a reliable horse should, Max responded to my verbal commands to walk, trot, or canter. Elizabeth picked up the rope again and he responded gentlemanly to her, too. He didn't strain to pull the rope from our hands. When I commanded, "Whoa," he stopped.

Together Elizabeth and I saddled Max. I considered asking Elizabeth to hold the reins while I got on, but I didn't. Instead of staying to watch, she escaped to the car to read, which I had parked in sight.

I put my foot in the stirrup and, as I was about to pull my other leg over his back, he took off. Fast. My right leg couldn't secure a position, it dangled somewhere between Max's side and his back. Still disconnected neurologically, my motor skills weren't functioning correctly. My brain could not respond with quick resolve. I couldn't think as fast; everything whorled wildly around me. I had experienced this with innocuous things, such as in counting out change, as my hands refused to move in ways my mind commanded them to. That this lack of control could affect a larger scenario hadn't occurred to me.

Max threw his hind legs out and up, twisting his bulk. He bucked again and again. When his head drew close to the ground, I could smell the dirt as he jostled me up and down, my pelvis and belly hitting repeatedly on the saddle horn. My left foot still in the stirrup, the right jiggled here and there. My hands could not grasp the saddle, or his mane, a move that would have given me some stability. I did not think to pull up hard on the reins. Then we parted. I landed on my head. My neck turned. Dust puffed into my face, my mouth. My legs came along like extra belongings that Max threw out.

Immediately, a severe headache and dizziness set in. Yet, I retained consciousness. Double Elizabeths stood over me, holding my glasses. "Are you okay, Mom? I saw what happened from the car."

I came to my knees where I stayed for a bit, my head hanging. "I'm okay."

When my eyes could focus again, I stood and put on my glasses, looked at my daughter. Her irises sparked out like frozen flower petals. Max stood a short distance from us. I wiped my face and mouth with both hands and moved toward him. "I'm getting back on him. But first I'm going to longe him again. I need your help." I took his reins. I wanted to yank on his mouth, to whip him with the reins, to kick him. Even if I'd had the strength to do this, though, I couldn't have. Violence kills the spirit. My rage belonged to me, not to Max. I changed his bridle back to the halter, not taking the time to remove the saddle. I ran him on the longe line until a pungent sweat soaked him. The anger gave me a resolve I'd not known I had.

"Whoa!" I called to Max and he pulled up and stopped.

"Elizabeth, hold him. I'm going to get on."

"I don't want you to, Mom." She stood between Max and me.

"There's no other way. It must be. You can't let a horse think he's won." I felt compelled to show her that this mom, whom she purported to despise, had some stuff. "You can't give in or life will defeat you," I said to her, picking up the reins.

Elizabeth held Max by the bridle. I took a deep breath. Slowly, I lifted my foot and put it in the stirrup. Just as slowly, I put my other leg over the saddle. I found the other stirrup. I took the reins. I sat for a moment, patting Max's neck. Once again, every part of my body hurt. My headache worsened. I took a deep breath.

Smashed by a semi, smashed by a horse. What did I have to fear?

With my tongue to the roof of my mouth, I made clicking sounds. Max stepped out softly. We walked until I felt comfortable. I turned him in the other direction and had him trot. We walked again. I said, "Whoa." He stopped. I could've ridden him, then, for hours, creating the bond Max needed in order to respect and trust me. But light-headed and weak, I could barely sit astride him. Carefully, I dragged my leg over and stepped down, holding onto the saddle for balance. We walked him to the barn. As we brushed him, every part of me trembled. I tried to hide it from Elizabeth, though Max detected it. Several times he turned his head to me, his ears neither cocked, nor laid back.

Elizabeth looked out the passenger's window on the way home. "I'm never going to ride him," she said to the pastures rolling by.

"Elizabeth, when he moved before I settled in the saddle, I should have dropped my foot to the ground, pulled down and around on the rein closest in. Turning him quickly would have stopped him." Then, realizing that Elizabeth had already shut me out, I said no more. I could only hope that, in that short space in time when her concern about me showed, my words and actions had made a healthy impact. What had my mother done when she couldn't get through to me? I had no idea. Many years had rolled by since she had died, and the dreams I had when she lived strayed far from any thought of ever having my own children.

At home, as I undressed to take a shower, I discovered the dark purple and black that spread from under my breasts all the way down to my thighs. My neck had stiffened. In a few seconds, I had destroyed eight months of physical rehabilitation.

In the months following the auto accident, doctors had injected me with vertebrae epidurals to reduce the crippling pain. Falling from Max brought on the need for more of these procedures. I wanted to ride that horse every day but falling from him had brought me to a new understanding: my body and mind refused to work in unison.

How my mother must have felt in those weeks and days before she died when pain controlled her.

The morning after I had impetuously driven to my aunts' homes, my mother sat up in a straight chair, her white hair wildly free, in a room away from her bed. She said, "I don't feel so well today." Dad and I repeatedly called her doctor's office, but he had not come in and his nurse didn't know how to reach him. Mom insisted she didn't want to ride in the ambulance to the emergency room. I sat in a chair with the newspaper in front of my face, pretending to read. In the early afternoon, as Dad read to her, she let go of her time on earth.

My own continuing grief and outrage lay above and beyond me, encapsulating me like a nefarious weight, and it prevented me from helping Elizabeth, whose wrath and sorrow overwhelmed both of us. Late one night, Elizabeth demanded to know where a library book had gone. It had been in the car for several days and so I had returned it, thinking I had done her a favor. But when I told her that, she screamed like a banshee, shattering what little inner reserve I had. I asked her to go outside so we wouldn't get into a physical fight. She went, and I soon realized that she had truly left. She had on a short skirt and no shoes. At first, I searched our property and then I began to walk the gravel road, but finding no sign of her, I went home. As I was about to call the sheriff's office, a deputy's car drove in our lane. The deputy said that Elizabeth and I needed to work things out. Elizabeth had walked to the blacktop highway and when people driving by saw her, they called the sheriff's office. A few days later, beckoned by an investigative social worker, I discovered that Elizabeth had told the deputy I'd locked her out of the house. I had already filled out an application to get her into a residential behavioral school and her running away helped to speed up the process. Shortly after her fall school term began, she went to live in a residential treatment center for adolescents.

Max moved back home after Elizabeth left. Sassy ran to the fence, whinnied and pranced like a young filly when she recognized Max. Before I could shut the gate behind Max, Sassy had moved along side of him, bumping shoulders with him as they trotted to the other side of the pasture.

One juvenile, Max, exchanged for the other, Elizabeth. While I visited Elizabeth every ten days and attended the therapy sessions at her new residence, I also hoped for the day when I could ride Max again. In time, Elizabeth could come home for two-day trial runs. The staff at the treatment center set up these stays to test her integrity. Any misbehavior that I reported to her therapist could be grounds to extend her admittance.

"I can't wait to work with Max and to take riding lessons," she told me when we sat in therapy. This comment filled me with the hope of collaborating with my daughter, of the two of us working together with horses. But would she honor what she said?

Seven months passed and Elizabeth returned home where she continued to push limits, though the threat of being returned to the school gave me leverage for who had the final say. I constantly worried about her, and each day I also pondered over what to do with Max. Elizabeth showed no inclination to work with him.

Soon a year had gone by since Max had lived at Amy's and he had not been ridden in all that time. The longer he lived with me, the fatter he became because I could not exercise him with the intensity that he needed. Horses need to be worked to keep their muscles toned. Max also needed to use his smart brain productively to prevent his attitude from growing sour. The thought of selling him daunted me. I grieved for everything, even for the horses of my youth. I admired Max's spirit, and I hoped that by keeping him I could gain fortitude from his company.

In my teens and twenties, I had rarely fought for what I wanted. The end product, whatever it might have been, appeared unattainable to me. However, now, as I coped to accept more deaths, I noticed that others had managed to achieve their intended goals, such as obtaining the desired job and marrying their soul mate. This seeming injustice, that others lived easily and didn't suffer numerous losses of loved ones, pummeled my senses. I had finally built my life to where I wanted it by moving to the country, having animals, and raising my children in a natural setting. But now, all parts of this life that I had worked so long and hard to attain eluded me. I had no idea how to hang on to my dream. To sell Max would be one more loss that I did not want to endure.

As I grew stronger, I took Max for walks on the road. He no longer reared up when on a lead. I let him graze in the yard. I also posted ads to sell him, pricing him too high, on purpose. After Sassy had moved in with us, I had a new stable built. There, I felt like a man with a new tool. I sat on the hay and soaped the bridles, the sweet scents surrounding me, the horses pushing their noses up against the doors to watch. Each day, I groomed them. Religiously, I cleaned the stalls. Each forkful I pitched out seemed to release inner tensions. Spreading out fresh pine shavings for clean beds freshened my soul.

After three more months passed, I made the decision to sell Max. Now six years old, he was too young to live a life doing nothing. I had to let go. Amy loaded Max into her trailer, taking him to a reputable sale barn. Tessa warmed him up in the outside area, as Elizabeth and I looked on. I had talked to Elizabeth about selling Max, had asked for her opinion. She had been noncommittal. "Do what you want," she'd said. Now, I watched Elizabeth's face, but I couldn't detect any emotion.

Other riders worked their horses. Some acted up. Some balked. Some were calm and did what they were told. Max fell into the last category. His walk was earnest, his ears forward. When his turn came in the sale arena, Tessa kept him moving and dancing. I stood by the auctioneer. Hands from the crowd came up here and there, none of them held high, but enough to indicate an interest. Soon, only two bidders continued to nod. Finally, the auctioneer pointed out a man in a blue-jean barn jacket sitting in front of me.

"He'll buy him, Ma'am."

I looked at the guy, surveyed him. Underneath his jacket, he wore a green-hooded sweatshirt, trying, like everyone else, to keep warm in the unheated arena.

"Gotta say fast, Ma'am. Are ya going ta let him go?"

The man had a kind, weathered and browned face. I nodded. Tessa rode Max out of the sale area and I followed, feeling detached. If I had allowed myself to enter the here and now, I would have crumpled into a ball on the earthen floor and sobbed.

Another man approached. "He ever worked with cows?"

I shook my head. My throat tight, tears too close, I couldn't stand it that I'd gone through with selling Max. I tried my best to keep a relaxed countenance, but I felt muscles screw up tight around my mouth and eyes, despite my intentions.

"Well, he will now! That fellow'll be throwing lots of ropes off this horse. He's going to a good home in Wyoming." I understood, then, that this man read the despair in my face and hoped to comfort me.

Amy saw my contorted face. In a soft voice, she said, "It'd be hell to sell one of mine."

With Max gone, Sassy whinnied, raced the fence line, called for him. After a few days, she gave up the frantic behavior. For two weeks, I couldn't go to the barn. After Max left, I had sunk to some place within myself, a hiding place like a tornado shelter. With Elizabeth at home, and returned to our district school, I trusted that she would tend to Sassy's needs.

Elizabeth went out at feeding times. Foolishly, I believed she had been doing chores. The first evening I accompanied Elizabeth to the barn, I found filthy water and a stinking, mucky stall. Sassy looked skinny. While I watched, Elizabeth stomped her feet and threw oats out, spewing them into the snow instead of pouring them in Sassy's feeder.

"Elizabeth! You've got to scoop that up. Feed it to her where she can eat it without working for it. She's an old lady and it's cold out there!"

"You fucking bitch! You do it," Elizabeth screamed in my face and ran out.

Within three months, Elizabeth would re-enter the treatment center and live there for seven more months, until the following August. I felt that since I could not control Elizabeth's behavior, I failed in my role as a mother. And yet, I also felt liberated realizing I could come and go as I pleased, and a satisfying quiet enveloped the house. The animals relaxed. The cats and dogs stopped whining and begging for attention. When I brushed Sassy, her muscles didn't seem so tense.

Caring for Sassy again became my ritual. I fed her and groomed her, cleaned her stall daily, gave her extra bedding when the wind blew high and bitter. Sometimes she turned her backside to me, squeezed me into the side of the stall, or refused to come in from the pasture. Eden, a neighbor and farrier, came to trim Sassy's hooves. I held the lead. Sassy shoved her hind end over, reared a little. Irritated, Eden grabbed the lead from me, yelled at Sassy, who knew that fear and indecision controlled me. Being a gentle old soul, she did not present the dangerous behavior that young Max had displayed. Nevertheless, my demeanor unnerved her. I had still not regained confidence.

The impatience from both Eden and Sassy, however, encouraged me to assert myself. The next time when Sassy moved sideways into Eden, I pulled down hard on the lead. "Knock it off," I said. When Sassy shoved her hind end against me, I shoved her away. "Knock it off," I said. She turned her head and looked at me. After that, she stood compliantly and then I knew she accepted me as the boss.

So Sassy's life and mine proceeded. Grooming Sassy became a zen. With her, I had no wish to be anywhere else. Her smooth coat glistened. I inhaled her perfume and hugged her around the neck. She held her nose to mine. Her warm, pleasant-smelling grassy breaths encouraged me to savor the moment.

Meanwhile, Elizabeth, at discharge, had been given an ultimatum by the treatment school staff. They had insisted Elizabeth apply to a boarding school. Once accepted, they warned her that if she did not do well academically and behaviorally, she would return to treatment for her three remaining years of high school.

For the remainder of the summer, she moved home and took a renewed interest in Sassy. This time, I felt it to be genuine. Due to the heat, however, Elizabeth waited until dusk to spend time with her. I set up a fan for Sassy in the barn as the heat index set in at 110 degrees. I would have done anything to encourage Elizabeth's renewed interest.

Witnessing her complacency and willingness to engage with anything, especially with Sassy, revived my hope that Elizabeth could move forward into a positive future, that perhaps we might bond.

Even so, the inner nagging, the tumbling-out-of-control feeling, began. The same premonition that had preceded my mother's death and our fateful accident commenced to haunt me again. No visible reason presented itself, but I worried that Sassy might not have much time left. As a result, I gave her more attention, especially when I felt rushed. Advantageously, doing this slowed me down and warded off the looming sensation of impending disaster.

One night, Elizabeth decided to saddle Sassy. I stood in the barn while she tied Sassy to the stall. Elizabeth picked out Sassy's hooves, combed through the tangles in her mane and tail, and brushed her. Then Elizabeth placed the blanket on Sassy's back, plopped the saddle on and tightened the cinch. Sassy reared. She turned, twisted, and fell. Her head hung stretched out on the lead rope, her eyes shut. She gasped for air, but the rope had twisted around her neck, squashing her attempts to get up. I grabbed the end of the rope, but Elizabeth had not tied it in a slipknot and I had not checked, expecting that she would tie the knot as I'd taught her. A slipknot can easily be yanked loose. I grabbed my pocketknife and sawed at the halter. Elizabeth dug her fingers into the rope to loosen it. We finished and I gently set Sassy's head down. She lay still, gasping for breath. Elizabeth and I watched, barely breathing. I undid the saddle cinch. Sassy sat up. After a bit, she put her legs out. With some difficulty, she rose. She held one leg up. After a bit, she put weight on it. Elizabeth led her into the stall. We called Dr. Al, bedded her, petted her, and gave her moistened oats.

Dr. Al diagnosed a bruised and sprained hip. In the days that followed, we kept a close watch on her. We had not realized that the unbearable heat had worsened her breathing condition.

In the late afternoon, the day before Elizabeth and I left for a vacation, I cleaned Sassy's stall, put down new bedding, cleaned the water trough, gave her special treats, and posted instructions for her temporary caretaker. That feeling of a tragic outcome ran rampant. I tried to shake it off, checked the fences, the stall, everything I could think of to ensure Sassy's safety.

The next morning, we had a plane to catch in Chicago, and a four-hour drive to the airport. As I rushed to take the dogs to the Pooch Palace, I noticed Sassy lying flat in the pasture, far enough away that I could not see her clearly. I yelled to her but got no response.

"I'll go check on her, Mom." Elizabeth said. She had planned to stay home and finish with last minute packing.

In the noisy old pickup, and already on the road, I saw Elizabeth waving frantically from the pasture. I detected distress, but I worried that we were running late. I yelled back, "Call Dr. Al."

When I returned from boarding the dogs, Dr. Al met me at the gate. Looking at his face, I knew. Quietly he said, "Your horse is dead. And there's only one thing I can think of that could have done it. Come look at her." I followed him. Elizabeth stood near Sassy's body, not far from the barn.

My God. Ripped wide open, her bowels lay strewn. Broken ribs stuck out; a small hole ripped through the top of her back. Blood, now dried, spilled out all over the ground around her. "I can't think of anything else but that someone shot her," the veterinarian said.

I reached down and stroked her face, rubbed my hand along her soft coat on her neck, now stiff, and straightened her mane. I turned to the doctor, and asked, "What do I do?"

"You'll have to call a rendering service or have her buried here. The sheriff should come and investigate. I'll call him."

I continued to babble on, obviously in shock.

Elizabeth, alone, had found Sassy. I wanted to hug Elizabeth, to hold onto her, but she refused my offer of comfort. I walked the road, looking for evidence, though I had no idea what it might be. Eden, driving her farrier truck, happened to drive by. I waved her to a stop and told her. She took tarps from her truck and covered Sassy. Eden hugged me, then went to the house and comforted Elizabeth with an embrace.

After I made arrangements for Sassy to be buried where she fell, Eden urged us on. "You'll miss your flight if you don't go now. There's nothing else you can do. I'll let you know if new information turns up."

Hours later, as we parked at the O'Hare Airport, Eden called.

"Sassy wasn't shot. She rubbed on a steel post, part of a surround fencing that protected a young tree. Her repeated uses of it for an itching post bent it. Eventually, she rubbed so hard that she came down on it." Eden had followed the blood trail through the pasture, finding the unwritten story.

Eden didn't have to tell me any more. In all my worries about Sassy, I hadn't thought to check the fences that protected the trees in the pasture. I pictured the mare, making her way, as her insides spilled out of her, trying to get home to protection, to find help. Alone, she must have been so frightened. Preoccupied and absorbed with getting the dogs to the kennel, I had left Elizabeth alone to find our dead horse.

Once again, I had no words for Elizabeth. On our vacation, each night I tossed and turned while I listened to her do the same in her bed. One evening I said, "Elizabeth, let's talk about Sassy." But Elizabeth stared at me with blank eyes. Her mind had already tossed out any possibility of discussion. Instead, during the days in New York City, she demanded that I buy her expensive things. When I refused, she screamed from her depths. She beat on me with her fists. People stared at us. Embarrassed and tired of taking blame for everything that went wrong, I shouted back. Guilt bred inside of me, spawning exhaustion and anger. Already remorseful, and believing my negligence caused Sassy's death, my extreme reaction to Elizabeth's misery confounded my emotions.

Back at home, we found sympathy flowers from Amy and Tessa displayed on our kitchen table. News travels in small communities. Those who appreciate animals, the kindred spirits, empathize. Amy invited us to her place to ride, to be with horses that would have been good matches for both of us, but I turned her offer down. Memories of Max prevailed there and I wasn't ready to face them. Elizabeth continued to act out but not as volatile as she had during our vacation. At home, I got glimpses of her in a better temperament.

Then Eden invited us to see her new filly, Ruby. Witnessing new life restores optimism in a crumbling soul, I surmised, so we walked to Eden's. The Cedar River bends at her place and children were riding ponies along its banks. After Elizabeth and I admired Ruby and played with the other animals, a girl Elizabeth's age invited her to ride the appaloosa pony.

"Yes, I'd like to," Elizabeth said, following the girl inside the barn.

Eden nodded at me and smiled. Elizabeth hesitated before she put her foot in the stirrup, then she swung into the saddle. Her back straight, shoulders wide, she picked up the reins and held them like an expert. Her hands relaxed as her fingers wrapped around the braided leather.

A moment passed before she gave the slightest squeeze with her knee, and during that pause, I felt my heart beating rapidly beneath my scarred ribs. When the pony moved, its ears flickered back, then forward, attuning to Elizabeth's instruction, leaving even hoof imprints in the indoor arena sand. Elizabeth urged the little horse again and they broke into a trot, a bumpy, rugged gait, but Elizabeth lifted and fell with the saddle, evenly guiding them around the ring.

I stood tall and rigid, my arms crossed. But when Elizabeth squeezed one more time and raised the reins just a little in anticipation of a faster gait, they broke into a canter, circling the ring. I laughed. I leaned onto the rails in front of me and put one booted foot on the bottom rung.

Sand from beneath the pony's hooves spit out in soft frays until Elizabeth pulled back on the reins. "Whoa," she said and turned him around to walk in the opposite direction. When she circled around where I stood, I saw her eyes lit up like an amethyst when sunlight strikes its crystals.

An ache built in my stomach that traveled up my throat. If only Elizabeth would have taken this initiative two years before, we could have kept Max. And, had Max stayed, Sassy would still be living. She would have had a companion to relieve her itches. Elizabeth wouldn't have to go to a boarding school in a few short weeks. Thoughts of how things could be railed on in my head while the glory of Elizabeth's ride went unheeded.

I wondered, too, what my mother would have done if the powers that be had dropped these same convoluted problems into the fissures of my mother's emotions. She had suffered many losses and had many illnesses in her life. She did what she had to do. She stayed busy, reflected and prayed. For the time being, I, unlike my mother, had given up on prayer, doubting its value; so much pain had damaged my faith.

When I, again, concentrated on Elizabeth, Eden held the pony's bridle and Elizabeth dismounted. She flipped her hair over her shoulder in the way girls do when they're feeling competent and pretty. Eden said something to her, which I couldn't hear, but Elizabeth nodded her head and then raised her chin in a wholehearted laugh.

I knew, then, that our lives had to be as they were. Elizabeth had things she had to work out. And, obviously, I did too, or I wouldn't have wasted my time pondering how events should have transpired instead of capturing the good moments around me.

CHAPTER
Eight

DEAR CAT

The spring after moving into the country, when Jon and Raymond lived, the sound of gunshots and frenetic dogs awoke me one morning as the house slowly gathered daylight. Determined to find out who disturbed the tranquility, I took a walk toward the dead end of the gravel road. A kennel truck, the name lettered on its doors, sat on the road's spongy shoulder. Not far away in last year's cornfield where broken stalks silhouetted against the rising sun, noisy hounds gathered around two men. At least one held a gun. I couldn't see the other clearly. The one waving the shotgun shouted at me, "We're jest runnin' coyoteeees. We ain't shootin' 'em er nothin'."

Three years after the semi rear-ended our van, killing Jon and Raymond and leaving me with life-threatening injuries, my closest neighbors, Mary and Dan, sold their place to that man who raised hunting dogs to run coyotes.

I would come to find that he had an aggressive and contemptuous attitude. I gathered this from the first time I met him when he claimed that once his dogs were loose, he had no control over them. I thought that an excuse for his disrespect for others' property. This man's retarded social skills and his refusal to acknowledge limits led most people to avoid him. My other neighbors, all good people, came to refer to him as "your neighbor," as though he belonged to me.

After "my neighbor" (I will not give him a name) moved in, he immediately pursued me, jumping in his truck when he saw me outside and then driving the six hundred feet from his lane to mine. I'd duck into an outbuilding and ignore his harsh banging on the door. Only a pasture separated our places, mine being the first stop on the dead end road after turning from the main gravel throughway. In order to go anywhere, he had to drive by my place first. If I happened to be outside when he drove by, he'd wave in a desperate way, as one might in gaining the attention of a long-lost friend. He'd stop his truck at my lane and stare in my direction. Sensing that he'd be inside my life in a second if I returned his hello, or his waving hand, arm, and shoulder in reply, I refused to acknowledge him. Often, when I visited Jon's and Ray's graves across the road from my house, I would find him standing in his yard, watching me.

He was ugly. He had some rotted teeth and some missing. His face sunk in like that of a drug addict. An indelible sneer showed on his face and assimilated in his manner. Yet I've known others whose physical mars go unnoticed because something happy shines from within the eyes. The kind of people you'd want to know, the person who leads you beyond a pallid acquaintance, into a sincere friendship. But that was not this guy.

Just as the semi-truck driver's negligence had eliminated my family, this neighbor's predation did the same to my privacy and dignity. The prospect that he might harass Elizabeth and wipe out her healing progress raised my anxieties. I also thought it likely he might injure my animals, something my veterinarian's technicians cautioned me to guard against. They knew the man well and knew how he treated animals, as he used the same clinic that I did.

Elizabeth attended boarding school and she spent her breaks at home. On Christmas Day, she and I had been preparing dinner for guests who hadn't yet arrived when someone slammed a fist on the door, disregarding the doorbell. I peeked down the hall to find the neighbor gawking through a window. In a moment of indecision, I impulsively opened the door a crack. He shoved a box of Hershey's chocolates at me. Caught unaware yet wanting to be gracious on such a holy day, I said, "Merry Christmas," and shut the door. Of course, if I hadn't been still recovering from a massive head injury, and had more command of my reasoning, I would have been more direct with him.

Immediately, I regretted taking the candy. My instincts were trying to tell me something. For several days, it sat on a hallway table where I avoided it, imagining it tainted by an evil prediction. I contemplated sticking it in his mailbox but I couldn't decide whether or not to write a note to accompany it. And, if I did attach a memo, what would I say? A week later, one of Elizabeth's friends took it and though now out of sight, I imagined that it had sullied my home.

Shortly after Elizabeth returned to school, two good friends visited. "You need to move," they said. "Your neighbor was the first man proven by DNA tests in Iowa to rape a woman, and he served time for it."

I replied, "In town, I could live twenty-five feet from a rapist and not know it. Why give up what I love?" The information about his past did add another dimension, however, to my limited experiences about his stalking. Even before I knew about his prison sentence, I had dreaded the sight of this man, so I stopped my morning walks on the road.

Years before, I had lived in southern Arizona, outside the village of Tumacácori, where I rented a cottage from a man who hunted. I taught high school then and in the early mornings as I got in my car to drive to work, I saw bobcat skins hanging from laundry lines and smelled burning flesh. I found it repulsive, even diabolical, to crucify sovereign lives for personal gain. I still feel haunted by those sights.

My neighbor disturbed my paradise in such a way. I had intended my fenced land as a haven for animals, wild and domestic, conserving four acres of lowland and trees where I would not pasture the horses or the sheep. I planted more trees and allowed the sedge, bristly foxtail, and cattail grasses to flourish. Barred owls, blue birds, warblers, titmice, finches, meadowlarks, all nested there. Mice, rabbits, and deer inhabited the field. A few times I came upon a fawn curled up, tucked tightly away in the long grasses. I had also sighted flocks of turkeys, lone hedgehogs, and families of raccoons, as well as squirrels, snakes, skunks, and the scat of coyotes.

From the ridge to the east of the house, where in summer the early mist slowly dissipated and the diurnal animals emerged, I could observe the shifting light throughout the day, grasses undulating like rippling water and the trees' shades rotating, like a sundial. In winter, sun reflected a luminous allure on the snow and when the wind lifted, fine sprays glinted against the blue sky like tiny crystals. Against that white background, I might see the tawny movement of a deer, or a succession of flying red, that of a flock of cardinals.

Here, I walked, circling, staying close to the fencing, in lieu of the two-mile daily walk on the road. Raccoon tracks printed the snow along the cattails, the continual passage of deer bared narrow trails, and owls peered at me from the crux of tree limbs. At first, I felt soothed, accepted as a member of this extended family of wildlife.

But the neighbor's pursuit continued. The desolation stuck in his eyes and his obnoxious attitude crushed me. I began to feel strangled, every move I made scrutinized. It seemed the wildlife felt the same. The coyotes' songs occurred less frequently and further away, down river. The barred owls that once inhabited my trees moved on. The flocks of wild turkeys dissipated. It even seemed that fewer bald eagles flew high overhead. Turkey vultures began to hover. The stench of unkempt dog cages drifted into my yard when the North Wind blew.

The spring following his gift of chocolate, he mowed the ditch from his house right up to my gate, chopping off the iris, day lilies, and narcissus I'd planted. He mowed so short that a dust cloud surrounded the twirling blades. Then, he began to mow there each week, eventually causing weeds to take over in place of my flowers and ornamental grasses. One day, I walked out the lane and waited for him, and when he shut off his machine, I asked him to not mow there because he had ruined my plantings. His dull gray eyes bored into me. Instead of answering, he started up the mower and continued where he left off.

Another time, as I looked behind me to back up the riding mower, I discovered him sitting on his mower waving frantically. Startled, I immediately faced forward and quickly engaged the accelerator, puzzling over what to do about his insidious audacity, and hoping he'd disappear. But he didn't, at least not immediately. He continued to watch me for some time until I finally stopped mowing and escaped to the house.

Not wanting to start an argument, I continued to retreat from these scenes. But, as encounters with him multiplied, I began to feel power-less, an emotion intensified by wondering if my thin skin had been predestined by genetics.

On both sides of my family, aunts, uncles, and cousins had diag-noses of depression. I learned of these troubles by eavesdropping on adult conversations. Clandestine meetings held at the kitchen table over coffee while I hid in the shadows of the walled-in stairs that led to bedrooms where I should have been sleeping. I gathered that the phrase "mental illness" described a shaming emotional pain and some-thing to whisper about only among the closest relatives, never to be mentioned to anyone else.

I prefer solitude to a constant trample of visitors. I enjoy reading, drawing, and the company of farm animals. When younger, other girls my age who feigned dress-up tea parties found me odd and tried to pressure me into playing "baby" by placing a doll on my chest and telling me to hold it. This action seemed so unreal to me I thought it resembled a Hitchcock movie. To hold a kitten and nurture it with soothing sounds and pets moved me, as did riding a pony, and stroking a newborn calf. But after other children taunted me, I began to wonder if I had inherited the unspeakable genetic defect, suggesting an abnormality in my makeup.

By the time I became an adult, depression had become a common term, and mental illness, redefined as brain disorders, roused the atten-tion of educators and parents. After reading its characteristics, I suspected I might have it. Not because of my penchant for animals, or a desire to create rather than attend a party. Rather, I waffled in decision-making, had difficulty concentrating, and dreaded new situations.

After I married Jon, my energy level began to drop. At the time, I realized I had encumbered the work—physically and emotionally—of two people. Jon had a lackadaisical approach to chores, and he brushed aside my wishes. I liked to dream about what we could do to our backyard, if we had the money, for instance. Jon would respond negatively, "It'll never happen," or "That's stupid." Soon, I wondered if my playful attitude was a fault. Eventually, after Jon repeatedly suggested I had an absurd character, I felt my creativity had been suffocated.

Under my physician's advice, I began taking an antidepressant. The doctor said that to receive its full benefit I had to take it for six months. After that amount of time, I stopped due to the negative symptoms of weight gain and fatigue. I felt worse than when I'd begun the drug. For a time, I believed the doctor who told me that because of my family history. Then he suggested I should continue trying other prescriptions. So, I maintained that depression caused my physical and mental condition. But no matter what I took, I intensely disliked the side effects and ultimately quit.

When Jon and I adopted Elizabeth and Raymond, the same physician stated I had symptoms similar to postpartum depression, caused by the onset of a new situation that entirely changed my life. I allowed him to, again, prescribe another antidepressant, hoping my energy would improve, as he assured me it would. Instead, I became groggy and irritable. My appetite kicked in and I gained weight.

The doctor explained that matching an antidepressant to a person's chemistry entailed experimenting with the medications until a particular one worked for an individual, in other words, a game of chance. But I tired of being a guinea pig and I didn't want to try anymore. Instead, I read about brain disorders and how the brain functions. Environment frames moods, I discovered. Yet, I didn't know what to do to change my conditions. I had two children who didn't do well with adjusting to new situations, either.

Then the accident befell us. Doctors in the hospital warned that without a mental mood aid I might be fine for months, but something could trigger an undoing. I stayed on a prescription for several months. I don't know if that medication proved effective because I was healing from multiple head injuries, among other impairments. All actions, thoughts, and feelings muddled together in my mind. Nevertheless, I had stopped that drug well before the new neighbor moved in.

Now with a Machiavellian character encroaching on my independence, I became moodier. My chest felt heavy and concave like a sinkhole where the earth's minerals have been dug out from below.

On my morning walks where I went around and around my own pasture, my imagination ran freely. I adopted the persona of an American Indian sent to a reservation. I tiptoed on the soft earth and hid behind the trees when the neighbor's truck drove by. Peering from behind the tall cattails, I supposed how a mountain lion might react locked behind bars. I could only presume through my own situation another's anguish from oppression, yet I could deeply sympathize.

The purpose of my walks transformed from exercise and observation to an unleashing of rising anger. I forced my feet forward, marching, and hurrying. I ran to rid myself of frustrations, to calm pulsing bodily sensations. I reacted physically to the snuffing out of my pilot light. I had worked so hard to keep a fire lit in my inner sanctuary after suffering the deaths of loved ones. I had created the haven for the animals as a means to retain my own existence. I adored animals, felt consoled in their company, and seeing baby animals play inspired joy that I didn't otherwise experience. Observing older animals in different modes made me grateful that I had survived, that I could see colors, hear voices, and smell.

Yet, I despised that someone, such as the man down the road who had such disregard for sentient existences, could foul my autonomy. Still, I feared that my personality caused some of the strife. I did not know how to confront a problem, any problem for that matter, but specifically this man who refused to leave me alone. As a result, I sought information, convinced that educating myself in any subject could resolve the problem. By delving into my books, I attempted to regain my repose. One essay in particular grasped my attention, Edward Hoagland's *Hailing the Elusory Mountain Lion* (1973). In it, he speaks of man's dualism, the fascination to *see* a mountain lion and the compulsion to *dominate* one. He writes:

In fact, at close quarters [the mountain lions] seem bewildered. When treed, they don't breathe a hundred-proof ferocity but puzzle over what to do. They're too light bodied to bear down on the hunter and kill him easily, even if they should attack—a course they seem to have no inclination for.... Although he could fight off a pack of wolves, he hasn't worked out a posture to assume toward man and his dogs.

I imagined myself as Hoagland's mountain lion, roped and dragged from a tree. Bewildered and in despair, my legs pulled out from underneath me, the forest's pine needles sticking in my fur, my muscles rippled then torn from the violent jerks of the ropes.

I'm not one to explain what goes on inside the head of a mountain lion, I've not seen one outside of a zoo. But humans' intense pursuit must baffle her. Perhaps her inertness at the sight of these strange beings, as Hoagland described, originates in her need to be left alone.

Hunters tenaciously pursue the mountain lion. So many hyperbolized stories pass from one mouth to another about wolves, bears, and mountain lions abhorrently killing domestic animals. Do hunters tell these stories to justify killing? To boast? The need to control possesses humans to physically annihilate another life in the same manner control causes humans to oppress and mutilate another's spirit. Such calculated torture.

I tucked Hoagland's words into my mind to contemplate. My neighbor obviously needed to suppress others, such as women and animals. Meanwhile, human friends, my domestic animals—the dogs, sheep, alpacas, and cats—and writing filled the hours after attending physical therapy several times a week. I had also begun to come out of my shell by serving on the local school board and volunteering at the animal shelter.

Though Elizabeth went to a boarding school, she had constant emotional needs, and sometimes I needed to drive the four hours to her school to participate in her therapy. When I left home on these excursions, I could not stop thinking about what the neighbor might do to my animals, and what he did do to any wild ones. I even worried about his confined dogs that he only let out from the small kennels for an overnight chase.

I investigated reporting him, but I had no proof that he ran an illegal puppy mill, though I saw him load his truck every few months with puppies and haul them away. He would tell other neighbors that he had a dog show to attend. On Sundays, he set up target practices in another neighbor's pasture, where only I could see him from my north-facing windows. He could not legally own or use a gun since he'd been a felon. But would I report him? No, I didn't want to risk his injuring my animals.

Then one night I dreamt of a mountain lion. Curled up on the sofa in the house where I grew up, her tail tucked easily around her. The sofa offered her a place to rest and restore her equanimity, an escape from past pursuers. Her raised brows formed wrinkles across her soft forehead, the way my mother's used to. The mountain lion contained an old soul's wisdom; her golden eyes simulated the same compassion as the eyes of my husky dog, Sasha, and a cat, Spotty. Both had died, but in life they had been my constant allies.

Suddenly, someone shot at the lion. She prowled from room to room, hissing and snarling. I, who had been watching her from the kitchen doorway, moved to a dark corner, frightened by her change of mood and by the gun. Then the scene changed. She moved through pastures and forests. I followed her. Sometimes she followed me. We met again underneath a trellised archway covered with thick branches of bittersweet, a place that had existed on my childhood farm. The lion then enigmatically collapsed there on a limestone walk and died in the fallen yellow and orange leaves of autumn.

I awoke, troubled by the dream's violence. I got up, checked on each animal that lived in the house with me. They all slept. I had sheep and alpacas and I walked outside in the dewy night air to check on them. Satisfied that all slept peacefully, I returned to bed. In slumber, the same dream reoccurred, although this time the mountain lion awoke, stretching her front paws far in front of her. She purred, raucously rubbing her big head on the old bittersweet trunk. I saw no blood, no gunshot wound.

The big cat of my dream puzzled me. How could she go through a horrendous ordeal and show no scars? Where did she originate? Who was she?

The trellis grown over with bittersweet in the dream had been in reality a creation of my mother's. The thick-trunked plant, lush with leaves in summer, abundant with orange berries after the leaves fell, resembled life, she'd said. We're all given something sturdy to begin our trek, and with it the propensity to grow freely. Later, as our vigor decreases, we are left with the fruits of remembrance, bitter and sweet.

With the tragedy of the accident, the lushness of both Elizabeth's and my lives had fallen on stony ground. In our own ways, we searched cautiously to find renewed meaning, to discover optimism.

During those first few months of my dilemma with the neighbor, Elizabeth, in her junior year of high school, tested for Attention Deficit Hyperactivity Disorder (ADHD), which her psychologist confirmed. In fourth grade, Raymond had been diagnosed with ADHD. I had researched the disorder specifically to understand his behavior. Accordingly, for Elizabeth, I read about it again and found distinct behavior traits that reminded me of my dad and my brother Mark (both deceased by then). Discovering that symptoms often resemble depression fascinated me, as did the fact that the two disorders can exist together.

When I told my nurse practitioner that maybe I had ADHD and not depression, she eyed me with doubtful authority, but she allowed me to take a simple test of several questions to which I answered *yes* or *no*.

"You have six categories! Four is the amount to recommend you for an evaluation!" She said and wrote a referral.

In the psychologist's office, during each of the five one and one-half hour tests, and especially when listening to a narrative and attempting to recall its content in sequence, I developed a severe headache. Upon finishing each session, I went home where I fell into a deep sleep. When I told the psychologist about the fatigue and neuralgia, she pointed out that I have to work much harder to stay focused than the average person does. This accounted for my exhaustion in so many situations that demand more concentration than I am capable of.

Focusing, an arduous task, can cause me excruciating head pain.

Sitting in meetings, for example, guarantees a struggle to listen and retain what took place. When I taught high school, I couldn't relax as some teachers advised me to do. Being constantly on stage and vigilant exhausted me in ways that didn't happen to other teachers.

I've been told that I don't hear well, but the crux of it is that I often think about other things when someone talks to me. Things I need to do, or something I recently read, or any number of ideas that may be developing to busy my mind. One might think that I could just turn this off and concentrate on the matter at hand, but no, I cannot.

In school, my mind had wandered off while the teacher gave directions. I survived by observing what others did or said immediately before my turn. Try as I might to catch up by tuning in to other students as they participated in the activity, my attention would invariably wander off again, and always without any indication. Something, perhaps the sound of the student's voice next to me, would snap me back to the immediate, always in the nick of time. Fortunately, I had the wit and quickness of mind to figure out what I needed to do to participate. Occasionally, I had to say, "Sorry, I wasn't paying attention."

If someone had asked me to detail what had transpired over the course of a class time, I couldn't have, unless I'd been able to take notes or doodle. Keeping my hands busy helped me concentrate. Reading or doing anything that I enjoyed kept my attention. Even PE class kept me present in the moment, though an athlete I was not.

A typical ADHD person needs constant stimulation. Creating and recreating, recalling and rehashing persistently bombard the psyche, causing anxieties. Obsessions about what to do with my neighbor dominated my thoughts. But learning that I had a brain disorder helped. I saw myself differently, gradually realized that I had worth, that my feelings and opinions counted. I began my long walks on the road again. I stopped hiding each time I saw his truck.

Summer arrived. Fed up with his presumptive intrusions, especially his mowing my ditch, I left a message on his phone saying, "I'd appreciate that you stop mowing my ditch. You are mowing irises and other things I've planted." I intended to be pleasant but couldn't control an edge in my tone.

Within a half hour, he drove his four-wheeler to my lane, his aggressive terrier running along. Barging through the gate on foot, dog at his heels, he beat on my front door. My dogs usually grew unruly and boisterous when another dog came on the property. This time they sat quietly on the inside of the door while I stepped out, closing the door behind me. Outside, my neighbor waved his arms and his hands. He spit on my front porch, almost hitting me with it.

"I'm a good man. I wave. I help you." Then he asked who was I to say he could mow my ditch, or not? He'd given me chocolates for Christmas. How could I not like him when he'd done that? If he'd made me unhappy, why didn't I tell him?

"I never asked you to help me," I said.

He stared at me with flat, gray eyes.

Something about his inflated sense of self-importance kept me calm. Until I fixed all the holes in my fences, I told him, his dogs marked all the doors on my house.

"You should have told me. Anyway, my dog that died did that."

Hmmm. Did he know his dog did that? I wanted to say, *what about the wood that's pried out of my back door and the nails left on my steps. Did your dead dog do that, too?*

"Where is it?" He then asked.

"It?" I asked.

"The boundary marker," he said. "What marks your land?"

As if he could not tell the difference between my yard and Beth's pasture. I pointed out the two old railroad ties used as corner fence posts. Grumpily, he agreed to mow only to the corner post.

The next time I walked past his house, he came to the end of his driveway. "Ma'am," he called out, "I've been thinking I know why you don't like me. It's because of what I did twenty years ago."

I continued walking. "Ma'am. Come here. Please, Ma'am. I have to talk to you about this." Behind him, on their porch stood a woman, whom I discovered later, lived with him.

I waved him off trying to indicate that he should forget it and let it go. I wished to be far away from his unoccupied eyes. I wished only to be left alone.

My wishes went unheeded. He continued to stop on the road and stare at me when driving by. But he had also begun to release his terrier, an unfriendly dog, when I walked. The dog would run out to the road and nip at my legs until I turned on it and stomped my feet, telling it to go home.

Each time he mowed, he swiped a little further into the ditch on my side. Poison ivy, burdock, Canada and bull thistles had replaced my ornamental grasses and bulb flowers, all because he had scalped the earth. Periodically I set up electric netting to corral the sheep in the yard so they could trim the grasses and weeds without eating the flowers. I had also begun to stake out sections of the ditch. Allowing the sheep to graze saved me from using chemicals to kill poison ivy, which grew in abundance. Staking out the netting was an arduous task, however. It tangled easily and the unsnarling took time. Sometimes I couldn't get the electrical current to run and that meant not putting the sheep inside it, as they would quickly figure out that nothing held them.

One intensely hot Saturday, again after summer and after Elizabeth had returned to school, I assiduously placed the netting, adjusting it to the ditch undulations. Because of the netting's length, which can't be shortened, a portion of it extended onto Beth's ditch. I connected the electrical current but couldn't get it to work. After five hours, overheated, frustrated, and fatigued, I escaped to the shop to work on another project.

In late afternoon, I heard my neighbor's mower. The volume increased, alerting me that he neared my property, where he should have turned back to his yard. But the mower stopped. Instantly, before I had time to think what I might do, I was out the door, out the gate, walking swiftly. He had ripped out the netting and threw it into a tangled heap. Already back on the mower, he headed home. I broke into a run and caught up with him. He swung the mower around so that he faced me and shut it off.

"You know, it took me a long, long time to set up that fence. You *are* going to set it back up, right?" I could feel my flushed cheeks and my entire body trembled.

"Hell, no!" He sneered. "You ain't got no right. Ditches are public property and you think you can do anythin' you want. I'm makin' it look nice."

"If you're so damned concerned about making it look nice, then why don't you mow the ditch on the north side of your place, or the one across the road?" I pointed at those places.

"You jus' don't like me and I know why. It's because of what I did twenty years ago."

"I don't give a shit what you did. I don't like you because you harass me!" I yelled.

"Harass you! I'm nice to you."

"You harass me, you invade my privacy, you slam on my doors, mess with my property." With shaking hands, I punched in the number for the sheriff on my cell phone.

"I gave you chocolates for Christmas!"

"I NEED someone here! NOW!" I said to the dispatcher on the telephone.

I stood on the road, waiting for a representative of the law. A sheriff's deputy arrived a half-hour or so later. The neighbor had gone home. Still irate, I explained what had transpired. The deputy drove up the road and I watched the two men talk, an exchange I'll never know about.

When the deputy finally returned, he said, "Don't worry. He won't bother you."

I had not intended to pounce on my neighbor, but observing and studying him for so long, combined with outrage at his gall, provoked an impetuousness that surpassed reason. I perceive my action as something cat-like; the mountain lion's deliberating pose before springing for her kill. The moment of her leap triggered by something deeper than cognizance. If planned, she might miscalculate the exact moment. For me, however, unlike after a mountain lion's kill, a tenacious vigilance set in.

In the nights, sleep came in short bouts. During the days, the fear of what he might do during my absences increased. I stayed close to home, again feeling trapped. After a week of frenzy, I confided in a therapist. There, tears of relief, of defeat and of sorrow burst out, like electrical currents fully charged. She suggested that I continue walks past his place to show him he couldn't control me, to work in the yard regardless of how he watched me, and to have a no-pass warrant placed on him. I needed to engage the powerful warrior, she said.

The powerful warrior appeared in my dream: Mountain Lion.

I'd shoved her out, rejected her guiding luminary. All those years of wasted energy, projecting another generation's depression onto myself, forgetting I was a person in my own right. Coming close to death and losing loved ones over the years—humans and animals alike—had made me acutely aware of life's fragility. I cherished privacy, repelling intrusive louts who disturbed my soul.

Learning at that age that I had ADHD turned into a curse and a blessing. A curse because I had been reduced to a label, and I rehashed the mistakes in my life due to impulsivity and the inability to focus. The lack of self-confidence had caused me to continually second-guess my liberty. Not believing in myself had allowed the neighbor to sense my faltering and thus move in on me. Yet despite the neighbor's irrepressible hunt, I had retained my prowess.

The blessing, however, came with the strength. I knew, finally, the mountain lion of my dream had been me. I had watched myself, a target for anger and control. I ran, hid, and nearly perished. But the cat rose again, her wounds mystifyingly vanished, evil discarded. My resilience actualized.

As for the neighbor, my attorney filed a no-pass warrant with the sheriff's office. To my favor and comfort, the neighbor's employer used the same attorney as I did. However, the neighbor continued to mow the ditch exactly three feet over the property line. When I worked outside and he drove by, I witnessed him shouting loud enough to raise my dogs' hackles. They would run along the inside of the fence line, snarling, until his truck surged forward, out of sight down the road. I ignored his attention-seeking behavior. As long as I kept quiet, I had the upper hand. He no longer came onto my property, and no longer tried to talk to me. That I appreciated. However, his presence had tainted my dream of creating a place of solace.

Yet his dogs, barking and crying day and night in their pent-up spaces, continued to disconcert me. Once, I went to the county sheriff's office and filled out a complaint, but as far as I know, no one came to inspect his place.

I planted more trees—ones already in heights of seven and eight feet, such as poplars and white firs. I could do nothing to protect the disintegrating wildlife population, though.

My other neighbors, those within the immediate vicinity, did not share these same concerns. Many felt that coyotes, skunks, raccoons, and others menaced crops and livestock. Neighbors who better understood the nature of wild critters and who did not find them an imposition simply had no time to involve themselves with my cause.

In the end, I tired of the constant vigilance. Five years had passed since the crushing of my family's van. I began to wonder if my physical energy would ever fully return. I wondered if I had taken on too much in attempting to maintain eight acres, its buildings and animals. When I had initially decided to stay in the country, I had wanted to keep the place for Elizabeth, as well as for myself. I had to prove to myself that I could heal enough to maintain the place on my own. But Elizabeth continued to express no real interest, and her help was sporadic and mostly careless. I had no concrete guarantee that if I kept the acreage she would appreciate it as an adult.

Elizabeth lived in a world of her own, and I had tired of dealing with our two different entities. I hired help from time to time and found I had to consistently supervise some of those who worked. Others would work a day or two and decide not to return, always leaving fences to be mended, or to be built, trees to be planted, gardens to be fertilized, all work that my body could not yet handle without undue pain. Neighbors would lend their time, but they had their own hard work and I felt embarrassed to ask them to spread themselves so thin. I had concerns that I could not take good enough care of my animals. I did not have the strength to grab a sheep by its front legs and turn it over backwards to clip its toes. I had no strength, nor quickness, to dodge the fleeting and powerful legs of the alpacas that I had purchased from a farm in Arizona, promised to be tame and gentle, but far from that.

I came to believe I would be better off in another place where memories of Jon and Raymond and my brother, Mark, animal friends, and other loved ones who had passed on would not haunt me.

For the time being, I curled up on the sofa. Took a nap.

Eventually, I would place a For Sale sign by the road.

CHAPTER

Nine

SEEING COLORS

P hil and I had danced in the streets of the French Quarter from mid-morning to evening in high spirits, slipping into countless bars, toasting my first Mardi Gras. Finally, in the late hours, I stretched out in the house where Phil lived, allowing sleep to anchor me.

At 6:00 a.m., Ash Wednesday, Phil stomped about the room, attempting to rouse me. "Let me sleep," I demanded, eyes shut. I had no desire to move.

Immediately, he took a flying leap onto the bed. Landing on his knees by my shoulder, he smooched my cheek. "Will you marry me?" Still on his knees, the bed wobbling, Phil produced a small box and presented me with an emerald, diamond-edged ring.

My eyes were open now. I sat up.

Though I'd had a crush on this man for twenty-some years, I had told myself I'd never marry again. But before I could consider his proposal, I accepted it. "Phil," I cried, "I'll marry you!" I grabbed him in a hug and pressed my lips to his.

At my age of fifty-four, Phil a few years older, choosing to marry this man should have been easy. Both Phil's and my parents had been deceased for some years and surely they'd have given us their bless-ings. But, when I accepted his proposal, I momentarily forgot I had an adolescent daughter, Elizabeth, who resented everything I did, and though far from capable of making sound decisions, she attempted to parent me. I had older siblings, too. One, my only sister would expect a good explanation for a major upheaval in my life. Phil's older brother, Mike, a worrier, would demand explanations from both of us. Mike and his wife, Ruth, had been two of my closest friends for nearly thirty years.

Phil, the younger of two in his family, and I, the youngest of five in mine, had not escaped the hierarchical sentiments of older siblings. We could be 150 years old and still be regarded as tots. Life, however, had served me a few nasty turns, and I believed in a turn at true happiness. Phil, too, had had his own trials.

With trepidation, I had booked this flight to New Orleans for an eight-day stay. Prior to the trip, my suitcase lay open for two weeks. I put pants in, took them out, packed a different pair. The same with blouses, sweaters, and shoes. I couldn't decide how to dress, or what I might need, even though I had spent hours on the phone with Phil asking him about the weather and what we'd be doing. Ears to the phone, eyes on the Internet, one thousand miles apart, we searched for Mardi Gras costumes. Snow swirled outside my Iowa windows as my dogs and cats curled up around me. Rain came steady at Phil's house in southern Louisiana. Phil chose a monk's robe. I chose a medieval Lady's dress, long and flowing, plenty of linen green material to take up my suitcase.

I packed and repacked and closed the suitcase the night before Mike and Ruth came to take me to the airport. At 5:00 a.m., I decided to change some items. When Mike and Ruth walked in at 6:00 a.m., my luggage rested in disarray, clothes lay everywhere.

Ruth said, "Oh my."

Mike said, "Jesus H, Jacinta. We've got to go."

Ruth helped me fold what I'd taken out. We put everything back and the suitcase wouldn't close. I sat on it and Ruth zipped it. Mike grabbed it and into the zero degrees we went, off to Cedar Rapids Airport.

Now, day seven with Phil, I didn't want to leave. I called home to arrange longer care for my animals, called the airlines and called Mike and Ruth to reschedule my pickup time. I would stay seven more days. Elizabeth, in a Wisconsin boarding school, assumed I was home. I hadn't told her about my plans to visit Phil. To date, each time I informed her that I'd be taking a trip, nurses at Liz's school would call, saying she had come down with some serious illness. I knew if I told her I planned to fly to New Orleans, she'd pull something to ruin my vacation. Elizabeth knew that Phil and I talked for hours on the phone. She knew I'd known Phil longer than I'd known Jon.

I first met Phil in the summer of 1986, on his biennial visit to Iowa City at a party that Mike and Ruth threw in Phil's honor. When I entered the tiny three-room cottage set in the woods, people milled about on the porch, in the living room and the kitchen, drinking beer and wine, gabbing on a Friday night. I bopped into one room, spotted the tall man with curly dark hair sticking out in all directions and took a step back. He turned and looked right at me.

"This is Phil, Mike's brother," someone said.

I nodded, attempted to say, "Welcome to Iowa," but the words caught in my throat. Suddenly I feared that if I said anything, I'd stutter. I slipped on by, grabbing a beer in the kitchen and escaped to the bathroom, curtained off from the kitchen, not far from the back door where several people congregated. I drank down the first beer, beat it to the cooler to retrieve another and re-entered my cave. I play-acted in front of the tiny mirror over the sink, primping my long auburn hair, practicing an opener: "What's so good about Louisiana?"

If someone needed to use the bathroom, I stepped out. When vacant again, I moved right back in. The buzz of voices from the kitchen penetrated the curtain and I heard conversations. Someone commented that Phil's wife hadn't come north and a pang hit my sternum. That he was married disconcerted me even more. I would not converse with a married man whose wife had been left behind. I also learned that Phil's occupation was woodworking, that he came to Mike's for occasional visits, and that he, too, had once lived in Iowa City.

"How disgustingly silly of you," I said to the mirror. After three or four beers, I finally left via the back door, walking quietly between groups of people, around the house to my car.

A couple of weeks after the party, I moved to Arizona to teach high school English and drama. Five years went by before I saw Phil again. By then I had married, and Phil had divorced. I had returned to Iowa with Jon and bought a house in a small town. Mike and Ruth bought a house a few blocks away, though our neighborliness came by coincidence, as neither couple knew the other had found a house there until after the offers had been accepted by the sellers.

Jon and I immediately began to renovate the kitchen. One humid, steaming summer day, Mike pounded on the heavy leaded glass of our front door.

"Phil's here for a visit," Mike said, pointing at Phil, who stood a head taller behind him. "I just wanted to show him what you've been doing, since he's a woodworker."

Jon led the way to the basement shop, and I tagged after the guys. Phil's presence relaxed me, allowing me to chat. I didn't talk so freely around Jon because he corrected most of what I said. As we all stood around the band saw, I dominated the conversation, detailing our adventures in redoing an eighty-year-old kitchen. We'd found signatures in the beaded cabinets, a toy tractor from the 1930s behind the sink, and an area that appeared as though fire had started in the oil heater's grate. Having elaborated for a few minutes, I felt Jon staring at me, his eyebrows scrunched, and lips set grimly. Excusing myself, I departed upstairs to wash dishes. Soon I heard Mike's and Phil's footsteps tromping up the stairs. I turned toward them, holding onto the sink's rim behind me. Phil nodded. He looked through me in the way someone does who connects with your essence, as if he saw inside my thoughts and feelings. I felt unnerved, yet unconstrained, something I had not felt in almost three years of marriage.

Phil visited every couple of years, at most. Each time, I went to the parties Mike and Ruth hosted, sometimes with Jon, sometimes not. I always took my two children, Elizabeth and Raymond, and sometimes my dogs. Phil and I greeted each other, but we never talked much. He walked past me with a "hello" and hurried on, perhaps thinking of my married status in the way I had thought of his years earlier.

One day, as I worked in the front yard, I noticed an unfamiliar car drive up my street's incline. Many cars passed by, but for some reason this one caught my attention. I gawked. Phil was driving it and he waved nonchalantly. Why, I wondered, did he choose to turn onto my street? Mike and Ruth lived on the next street to the east.

A couple of days later at Mike's and Ruth's party, Phil strode up to me and said, "You looked like a woman who just saw her lover from the past." Before I could answer, he spun on his heels, off to another room. I grinned at the audacious insinuation simply out of embarrassment. What nerve, I thought. Still, the attention intrigued me.

As friends do in conversation, Mike and Ruth occasionally mentioned Phil to Jon and me. In these moments, my husband Jon slipped into a heavy and uncomfortable silence. I never knew whether or not Mike and Ruth could detect Jon's tacit protest. They had been my close friends for several years before Jon entered my life and our exchanges remained candid. At one time, for the sake of conversation, I had reiterated to Jon what I'd learned about Phil, but Jon immediately shut down, his normal reaction when the topic of Phil arose. I began to keep information Mike and Ruth relayed to myself.

Then, in the mid 1990s, Phil spent a summer renovating Mike's and Ruth's kitchen. Occasionally, the children and I dropped in to check on the construction progress. Phil answered Ray's endless questions about tools. At summer's end, Phil moved to Bay St. Louis, Mississippi, setting up his own woodworking business. He stopped visiting Iowa.

Soon after, Jon and I moved to the country, ten miles from Mike and Ruth.

My job, farm work, and raising children preoccupied me until the accident. A few weeks after I came home from the hospital, Phil sent me *The Tibetan Book of Living and Dying*. Not knowing my address, he sent it to Mike.

I stood outside in the cold January wind and watched Mike and Ruth get into their car at my house. Like so many others in the community, they had come to help me with the animals and housework. Having head injuries, my bones and muscles not yet healed, I grappled with rejoining this world. I longed for cognitive and physical abilities that would eventually return. I hated depending on others to subsist. I waved as I watched Mike start the car. Letting it idle, he got out again and returned to me, with a book in hand.

"From my brother," Mike said. I felt puzzled, my face contorted. I thought, *Why from Phil?* And, *He's thinking about me?* Mike shrugged his shoulders as though in answer to my silent questions and the book gently fell from his hands into mine.

Back in the house, I sat down with the book. Inside its cover, Phil had tucked a card explaining, in his neat handwriting, how the book had helped him cope with his own losses. Over the weeks following my hospital stay and the memorial services, I had gotten many cards and letters, books and gifts, but none connected with me as did Phil's brief sentiments. I felt an inexplicable link to this man.

I could only read a page or two at a time before my head would ache. Limited cognitive functions and grief complicated my emotions, so I would begin to cry and then completely forget what I had just read. Then I would glance at Phil's card and be comforted, knowing he was indeed thinking about me. Eventually, I would interpret some meaning. We are given this existence to learn. After this flesh's death, the spirit continues its journey to attain full understanding. Our rate of spiritual growth determines how many times we will return in bodily form. This concept jibed with my belief. Some people thought I'd lost my marbles when I expressed these thoughts, but Phil obviously heeded the same notion. That he gave me the book boosted my confidence. It helped me work through confused thoughts, fear that might emanate from another's facial expression or verbal comments, or anything that might cause me to cry. It assisted in maintaining my sanity when feeling completely numb in one instant and turning topsy-turvy into rage the next. The vacillating could transpire in minutes. Despite all of that, I continued to pay bills, cook meals, help my daughter and care for the animals. I kept up with daily living, though not much made sense to me in those days. Except I knew I should be learning *something* from all this.

———

Time passed. Twenty months in total. At the end of August 2005, Mike called to tell me Phil had evacuated from Hurricane Katrina, and that New Orleans had drowned, as had many towns along hundreds of miles of the Gulf Coast, which included Phil's town of Bay St. Louis. Three days later, Phil arrived in Iowa. When Mike and Ruth brought him to my house, I recognized the distracted mood of the traumatized: his clenched jaw and wrinkled forehead. His mind, far from the moment, buried in the need to return home to find his cat, and to salvage what he could from Katrina's massacre.

I invited Mike and Phil to the shop where Jon's tools, after almost two years of disuse, lay. I hadn't the energy, or the knowledge to sell them. But Mike and Phil needed implements to clean up rubble, chop trees, saw and crowbar their way through the detritus of nature's wrath in Mississippi.

"How about this?" One or the other would ask, picking up a saw, a shovel, a hammer, or a chain.

"By all means, take it," I said.

I packed up Raymond's clothes and toys and added them to the growing load bound for The South. Raymond would have wanted to give his things to those in need. With Ruth, I stood beside the borrowed truck, its covered bed filled to capacity with supplies. In a few days, Ruth would fly to join them. Several weeks would pass before Mike and Ruth returned home.

Nearly three years would pass before I saw Phil again.

"Phil's coming," Ruth confided to me in early July, the summer of Senator Barack Obama's campaign in Iowa. "Mike doesn't know about Phil's visit. It's a surprise."

My vehicle had become our group's "Obama Mobile," transporting supporters from Mike's and Ruth's house, the central gathering, to hear Senator Obama. I didn't know exactly when Phil would arrive, but the day scheduled to hear the future President speak in Cedar Rapids became my day of surprise, too. As I slid out of my car at Mike and Ruth's, Phil walked out of the house. I offered him my hand in greeting, but he ignored it, instead pulling me to him and saying, "You deserve a hug."

He embraced me and released me, all in one motion. I took a step back and swallowed hard. He grinned mischievously. He waved me into the house, beckoned me to greet Clodell, his little black cat, then we joined the Obama devotees in the kitchen.

Most often, Elizabeth, when home from boarding school, went with me to Senator Obama's speeches. I still could not trust to leave her home alone, but on this first day of Phil's visit, Elizabeth had gone to her friend's house. Her absence allowed me an adult day, and a time to nervously—now that Phil had hugged me—ponder his new approach. It seemed we were no longer mere acquaintances, nor were either of us married, and keeping a safe distance from each other seemed to be in the past. We spent more time exchanging stories in these hours than we had in all the twenty-some years we'd known each other. He told me about wearing eyeglasses from age three, the trials of making school friends because his parents, theatre directors, moved frequently for better job opportunities, and other tales. I told him about my child-hood animal friends on the farm, and that set us both to relating stories about our pets.

A few days later, Mike and Ruth bought an extra ticket for Eliza-beth to accompany the four of us to a music festival. Elizabeth sat on one side of me and Phil on the other. Phil talked about playing the guitar and the washboard. He talked about his woodworking in refer-ence to the renovated theatre where we sat. I couldn't think of anything to say. I could have told him I had formed a group of people in the 1980s to save the Englert Theatre, built in 1916, where we were sitting.

I could have asked Phil what growing up around community theaters had been like, but I didn't say much of anything. After the performance, Mike, Ruth, and Elizabeth found acquaintances in the crowded evening streets. Phil and I stood side-by-side, leaning against a building, watching the others mingle. I tipped my head up at Phil, who with arms crossed looked at me like, *Well, I've tried talking to you.*

"What's up with your property in the Bay?"

"The wrath of God," Phil answered. "I haven't sold it and I have to look at what remains."

I understood the wrath of God.

Now, well into August, Phil had not yet gone home. He and Mike and Ruth had come to my house to look over more tools and equipment I wanted to clear out. When they arrived, I had clothespins in my mouth and wet towels in my arms. A vibrant country wind snatched the towel from my hand as I attempted to pin it on the line. Phil walked by with Mike, said, "Let's help this lovely woman hang up her laundry." He picked up the towel, hung it, and grabbed another.

On this day, my laundry day, Phil's attitude amazed me. Aroused me. Not only did he notice that I needed help, but he also actually assisted me. I had heard women describe knowing, that moment of epiphany, when soul mate made sense. Hanging a towel in the wind hardly seems romantic, but in that moment Phil became the most handsome, smartest, sensitive man I'd ever met.

Clothesline full, my hands shaking from my recent revelation about Phil, we walked the ten yards to the shop. Five and a half years had passed since the accident and since the tools had last been used, except for hammers and such that I'd used to mend fences or fix things on the property.

Electric drills, a table saw, a jointer, a Dremel set, many other implements and gadgets lay strewn inside the building. Since Phil expected to leave the following day, I bid farewell. I had other chores and I didn't intend to hover over his shop investigation. He had begun his visit by hugging me, so I embraced him now. We shared solidarity, knowing that hell lives on earth. Phil understood losing his life's work and people he loved due to nature's rage. I, too, knew loss on that grand scale. We both belonged to the scramble of survivors.

Mike noticed us hugging and piped in with, "Phil, why don't you invite Jacinta to visit you?"

"Yeah, when?" Phil asked.

"I don't know," I shrugged. "I've got a lot here that needs me." With that, I waved and left.

As it turned out, Elizabeth and a friend of mine had planned an early surprise birthday party for me before Elizabeth returned to school. Unbeknownst to me, Phil wouldn't leave Iowa until after he attended the party—until he and I had locked eyes from across the room of people and smiled at each other.

Phil left when I took Elizabeth to her boarding school for the fall semester of her senior year. As I, again, settled my daughter into Wisconsin, a mild hurricane arose in the Gulf waters. By the time I arrived home, Phil had returned, driving the one thousand miles back to Iowa. It was, as he said, to seek refuge from the storm. But I knew better because the storm hadn't reached a threatening category.

On a Saturday night, I cooked a dinner for the four of us. Phil sat at one end of the table. I sat down on the other end with Mike and Ruth serving as a buffer. I wanted to be next to Phil, but I couldn't relax. Phil had intrigued me for decades. All those years I had observed him, understanding through Mike and Ruth that he had a caring, sensitive, and intelligent manner. Yet, my own strong feelings unnerved me. What if I just had a girl's crush? What if we tried a relationship and it didn't work? What if...?

Neither of us made a move to admit our attraction and Phil returned to the South. I went on with preparing my land and animals for the Iowa winter and thought about him every day.

One evening at Thanksgiving time, I stopped at Mike's and Ruth's with Elizabeth. Other friends had stopped by, too. By chance, Phil called while we visited and Mike handed the phone to me so he could attend to other guests. Again, Phil asked me when I would come to see him. I didn't really know. We exchanged emails and within a week were communicating regularly through our computers, right up to

Christmas when Phil suggested we call each other. Our first phone call lasted over four hours. I hate talking on the telephone. I would rather sit down with the person. But with Phil, it felt as though he sat in the room with me as we told each other our life stories.

Every third or fourth evening, we talked into the wee hours. Elizabeth, during her winter break at home, complained that my laughter kept her awake. After she returned to her school, Phil began to call at 6:00 a.m., my wake-up call, also the start of my usual writing time. Soon, we conversed each evening, too. And then, on a Saturday in January, a blizzard swirling outside my windows, we talked for ten hours, breaking only for lunch and supper. Throughout this time, Phil had continued to urge me to make flight plans. Each time he would say, "When *are* you coming?"

Tomorrow, I thought. *Never?* Inevitably bound to be together, the thought of it frightened me, though I didn't exactly know why. Change threatened me—I'd had plenty of it already. The possibility of rejection intimidated me. Phil and I got along so well that I found it hard to believe a love affair could be so easy. Certainly, once he knew me better, he would begin to pick at me. I might irritate him. He would take to treating me gruffly. He might try to pass me in a narrow space and bump into me, blame me for being in the way. He might make me promises, such as a luncheon date or to help me with planting the garden and then not show up. We might discover that our basic ethics about life and people differed. Phil might not agree with my parenting methods. I had a plethora of reasons to be nervous, yet I felt without Phil I would fall back into the doldrums of mental and physical pain, that my life would be defined by the hell I'd lived through. With him in my life, I sensed a new beginning and for the first time in years, I knew what it felt like to see colors, and to notice the world outside of myself.

Elizabeth's spring break came in March, three weeks after my return from visiting Phil at Mardi Gras. On her first day home, I told her to pack her bag for a trip. The next day, Phil picked us up at Louis

Armstrong International Airport. After lunch, we went to *Promenade*, an Italian fabrics store on St. Charles Avenue. Phil and I had planned to tell Elizabeth about our engagement over dinner that night.

As I shopped for the perfect silk, Elizabeth said, "Why is Mom, who lives on a farm, looking for silk to make a dress?" Before either of us could say a word, she screamed, drawing the attention of everyone in the store.

"Oh! I get it. You're getting married. That's why I'm here."

As people in the store congratulated us, Elizabeth took over the show.

"I knew at Thanksgiving when we stopped at Mike and Ruth's and you went out on the cold porch away from everyone to talk to Phil that something was up. Then," she turned to the customers, "they talked all night long during my Christmas vacation, keeping me awake, Mom laughing like a high school girl," she said accusatorially, but I turned to Phil and smiled.

Weeks later, Elizabeth would say angrily, "I thought you two were just getting married. I had no idea he was going to live with us. And why would you want to *marry* him, anyway?"

She felt a loss of control over me—not that she ever had that—and she feared the changes. On the other hand, life for me with Elizabeth had no joy. Her wrath never ceased, whether expressed overtly or passive aggressively; she always aimed it toward me. I felt bad that her early years had stripped her of self-esteem, of the ability to love unguardedly. Yet I had given my maternal all to help right her life and she refused my care, detesting me instead. Ultimately, she drained me.

"Because he makes me laugh, Elizabeth," I said, replying to her question. "He makes me feel good about myself."

My mind wandered back to Mardi Gras. On St. Philip Street, Phil and I had slipped into a darkened storefront where candles and incense burned. A fortune teller had read my hand and reported, "You have had an unhappy life. Losses of loved ones. I see a little boy you loved very much has died."

I choked. How could she know that?

She softly stroked a line on my left hand with her finger. "But I see that your future will be happier. There is someone you are fond of who will stay in your life. You will be happy together, but it won't always be easy."

Phil sat in the back of the room. I watched his head crane toward us as the woman spoke, watched for his reaction but realized he couldn't hear her. I had noticed yellow in the whites of Phil's eyes, which concerned me. I wondered about his health. But choosing to believe love would overcome obstacles, I interpreted the psychic's caution as missing Raymond and the ongoing parenting of Elizabeth.

"What'd she say?" Phil pumped me as soon as we faced the sun in the street. But before I could answer, he said, "Did she say anything about a relationship?"

I laughed and repeated her words.

"Aha," he answered, taking my hand and pulling me back into the throng of costumes and cacophony. Life with Phil would be like this, I thought. I will hear distressing news and as I begin to digest it, he will grab me, turn me toward some kind of joy.

———

Less than two months after my first sojourn to visit Phil, we married in the office of the Justice of Peace in Iowa. Mike and Ruth and two other friends, Jim and Rosalie, stood for us.

Phil and I began planning a public wedding and reception for August while taking steps toward hunting for a new house in Louisiana. Soon Elizabeth would graduate from high school and be home for the summer. Phil made an appointment to get a physical exam. I began to sew my wedding dress.

I had chosen silk georgette, thyme green with a print of small red roses, finely twisted woven threads, lightweight and transparent. Although once a skilled seamstress, I had not sewn since before the accident. Now I made plenty of beginner mistakes. Silk slides and slips when pinned and cut. I didn't pin the fabric enough to secure the pattern before cutting it. In sewing the seams, I remedied the slippage, but the length turned out jagged, as much as four inches. Each time I tried to align it, I trimmed it more crooked. I had begun the pattern as a calf-length dress, but after several attempts to even it out, a few sections fell just below my knees. I stopped straightening for fear I'd have no more fabric. Instead, I rounded the squared corners, submitting to the uneven gypsy-like hem. The pattern included buttons from neckline to the hem. Even with interfacing and a thin needle, airy silk has a mind of its own and plays out where it will, no matter the precautions to hold it in place. Deft fingers and a light tread on the foot pedal help with the desired results, as does slow sewing and heavy concentration.

The dress became a metaphor. Each time I thought I had a grip on the direction of my life, no matter how arduously I worked to master it, a fragment slipped and slid, upsetting my foundation. This theme tailed me. The summer weighed in as a balancing scale. For each smoothly accomplished endeavor, another jacked up the stress factor.

Elizabeth continued to be non-helpful in general. At our insistence, she got a job but refused to learn to drive. Phil and I had to drive her thirty miles and pick her up later in the evenings. Then her employer fired her because she wouldn't do what he asked. Instead of looking for other work, she hid in her room except to eat, slung accusations, fabricated stories, and engaged in temper tantrums. I set up a plan for her to weed around one tree per day in the yard. She refused. I demanded that Elizabeth do something to earn her keep. In turn, she stood in front of me and yelled, "I'm not your slave!"

Phil came from another room and stood behind me and said, "What your mother asks is what needs to be done. You will not yell at her or challenge her."

Scorn crossed her face as she retreated with her shoulders hunched. She did not yell at me again in Phil's presence, but she flatly refused to do anything.

As Phil and I continued to arrange our reception, we listed my place in the country on the realty market. We also took care of other crucial items, including our medical check-ups. Four weeks after Phil's physical exam, our nurse practitioner requested a retest of his blood work. Shortly after, she informed us Phil had Hepatitis C.

Phil didn't immediately grasp the seriousness of the diagnosis. But I understood exactly what the prognosis could entail. I had watched my brother, Mark, gradually fail over the years and finally die a gruesome, painful death from Hepatitis. When I heard Phil's news, I lost my appetite and my spontaneous sobbing returned. I lashed back at Elizabeth when she spouted her anger. I lost sleep and couldn't focus on finishing our reception plans. Phil took over, telling me that all would turn out okay.

I didn't understand then that Hepatitis has different categories. My brother had Hepatitis B, for which there had been no treatment. Phil had Hepatitis C. He *might* recover, if his genotype concurred. Fortuitously, it did.

We also discovered that millions have Hepatitis C, which is a bloodborne disease. Phil could have been infected while cleaning up from Hurricane Katrina. Storm waters and stagnant debris contain various life-threatening bacteria and viruses. In the year after Katrina, Phil drove a chisel through his hand, landing him in an ER where he had a number of stitches. Some people have been infected in hospital emergency rooms. The virus can hide in a person's system for years before detection, but we speculated that Phil's infection hadn't been long-term, and that eased my worries about the damage to his liver and other organs.

Despite my concern over Phil's health, we successfully celebrated our wedding, speaking our personal vows in the open air of the Hoover National Historic site. That evening, as people gathered and took chairs, my heart began to beat erratically, upsetting my stomach. Phil's health tormented me. I hoped for at least thirty happy years together, but could we, given his medical diagnosis? I walked to the giant fireplace in the outdoor pavilion, my dangling dress hem sticking to my legs in the August humidity. I took deep breaths, straightened my shoulders, and coached myself. *Phil will be fine. Enjoy the evening.*

"Are you okay, Honey?" Phil had come to where I stood. Though looking relaxed in his umber and white seersucker suit and Panama hat, I knew differently. He'd been shouting out orders to the help, trotting to and fro, and checking on the reception's progress.

"I'm fine," I said. We walked to the oldest oak in the park, the one we'd chosen to stand under and openly pledge our love to each other. The thing to do, I thought, would be to allow this evening to continue forever. The slow summer night, the light breeze, a gathering of loved ones. Violin and bass players accompanied our poetic vows. Guitar and accordion music followed as people socialized, ate, and danced. Later, when the ambiguity of Phil's health and Elizabeth's behavior unfolded, I would recreate this scene in my mind as a reminder of better days.

Many things had to happen before the end of summer, and we managed to do them all. We sold my sheep and alpacas; packed up Elizabeth's belongings to ready her for college; put my acreage up for sale; and looked at houses in Iowa City where Phil's treatment for Hepatitis would begin in the next few months.

At Elizabeth's freshman orientation, we encouraged her to meet others in her dorm, took her to student services, talked with the director about Liz's challenges, her anxieties and her requirement for guidance. The small college had a reputation for monitoring students with special needs and helping them to succeed. I never knew what antics she might pull, but now someone else could keep tabs on her. I hoped she'd mature in the coming year. Meanwhile, I could let go and concentrate on Phil's and my next phase.

Once a week, I called Elizabeth and emailed her. I also sent her cards via the post office. She did not answer. I hoped for the best, that she had found friends and had gotten involved with school activities.

Phil and I returned to Louisiana to pack up Phil's belongings and bring them North. While there, I received a phone call from the director of student services at Elizabeth's college. She said, "Mrs. Kehoe, we have Elizabeth here with us. We must discharge her for this semester. She has not attended classes and has a serious medical problem. I'm sorry to relate this, but it is also after the date of withdrawing from classes without forfeiting your full tuition. It is October, after all."

Not at all surprised to hear that Elizabeth had a "serious medical problem," I asked what that could be as Elizabeth had feigned illnesses all her life.

"She has worked with our student health services and has been to the hospital several times for tests and overnight stays. She has abdominal pains."

My stomach flip-flopped. My face heated up. I sat down. Furious that these experienced educators would allow Elizabeth to snow them, I said, "Let me speak with her."

Elizabeth came on the phone. Her voice sounded crotchety and weak, a ploy she had used many times and I knew it well.

"What's the matter with you?" I asked.

"I don't know. I just don't feel well, and I have terrible pains. I've had tests and these show that my gall bladder enzymes are high."

"What?" I yelled into the phone. "Gall bladder enzymes? Did you ever think of calling me and talking about this? Did you get the messages I've sent you?" She had heard us talk about Phil's liver enzymes.

"No. Mom, I'm so sick."

"Yeah, right. You are." Impeccable timing. She knew I couldn't go there. She knew Phil's medical situation consumed me.

"I don't know what you're going to do with yourself. I can't come and get you."

"Oh, it's okay. Billy will come and pick me up. He says I can stay with him and his mom." Her voice lightened and she sounded perfectly well. My arms and legs vibrated, pumping blood.

"Fine," I said and hung up.

Intermittently over the next few days I called the college, requesting a tuition reimbursement. It didn't work. I had emphasized she was a challenge to herself and would be to anyone who encountered her. The officials suggested that she enroll in the January term and take one intensive class to prove herself. Now, where was she? She had left school after we'd spoken on the phone, leaving her belongings behind, and not giving a forwarding address.

With Phil's earthly possessions on a moving truck, we returned to the North. Immediately, I went in search of Elizabeth. Her friend, Billy, informed me she'd already left him for another fellow she'd met on the Internet.

We moved into our new house with the dogs and cats in Iowa City. Phil began to correspond with Elizabeth via email requesting she touch base with us once a week. She did. One day, a few months later, she called and said her boyfriend and his mom would like to meet Phil and me.

I had the insurance statements from Elizabeth's "illness" in my purse. I owed over $2,000.00 out of pocket and tossed the papers to Liz during lunch.

"That's a lot to pay to get out of going to school," I said. Insisting that Elizabeth pay the bill would simply stress me, as she would expertly dodge any responsibility. I brought the situation into the open to caution Josh and his mom, seemingly hardworking and normal. I couldn't speak frankly, however. I had become diffident since the accident. Confrontations frightened me.

An expert at changing subjects, Elizabeth said, "Well, I'm going to try again. Josh has talked me into going back and trying the January term. It's only $5,000, then I can enroll in second semester."

I looked at Josh and he nodded his head, smiling.

"Okay," I said, "I know you can do it."

In December, Phil began his chemotherapy regimen, the proposed cure for Hepatitis C. After dinner on a Friday, we sat in the master bath. Phil chose a spot on his stomach. He held the needle to his skin and closed his eyes. He pushed the instrument in, squeezed the syringe, pulled it out, and let go of a deep breath. I, too, exhaled. Silently we looked at each other. From then on, I kept a vigilant watch for changes in mood, behavior, skin color, and anything appearing unfavorable in Phil's demeanor and physical appearance.

Phil's brother, Mike, attended each bi-weekly medical appointment with us. In the exam room, a lab technician extracted eight vials of blood, and the physician assistant examined Phil's lungs and heart, general color, and anything else significant to his examination.

Every weekday he would swallow two pills of Copegus, also an interferon drug. Fridays became the weekly Pegasys injection day. After supper, he'd hold his head in his hands.

"What can I do for you?" I would ask.

"Tell me I don't have to take a shot." He would go to the fridge, take out a syringe, trudge up the stairs. After a few Fridays, he locked the bathroom door. "I don't want you to watch me," he said.

Phil came downstairs on Saturday mornings for breakfast. At first, he worked in his study, socialized, and helped me walk the dogs. In the afternoons, he napped. In time, he became weaker and had fewer good Saturdays, or for that matter, any days after the Friday night injections.

One night, towards the end of January, Elizabeth called. "I have three more days of J-term," she said. "I'm getting an A and my paper is due Monday."

"Fabulous, dear," I said.

Elizabeth talked about how she'd like to transfer, but she would continue and do the second semester while searching for another college. She soothed me for an hour and my worry floated away.

When Monday arrived, the same woman from student services I'd spoken to in the fall phoned.

"Mrs. Kehoe," she said and cleared her throat. The tone of her voice told me immediately that Elizabeth had pumped me full of nonsense again. My neck tensed. She continued, "Elizabeth left the dorm this weekend. Again, she left all of her things, then she emailed me this morning and said she won't be coming back. Maybe you can convince her otherwise. She had an A in the course, just needed to hand in her paper. In all my years of dealing with young people, I've never had the experience of someone like your daughter."

Had it been another time, when I had no other worries, when fatigue didn't plague me, I would have railed, and I would have given the woman a good piece of my mind. But now I merely said, "That's Elizabeth."

I did not try to contact Elizabeth, as I did not want to be snowed again.

Phil's belly filled up with bruises. He slept through more Saturdays, Sundays, Mondays, Tuesdays, and Wednesdays. By Thursday, he could move around, sit in a chair, and maybe read. And then with Friday's shot, the round began again.

Two weeks after Elizabeth left school, she called me.

"So how did you manage to get a ride?" I inquired.

"Josh came and got me. I was crying because I just didn't think I could do it."

No doubt she pumped the tears. Josh surprised me, however. He'd soon graduate, and seemed to realize the value of an education. He'd had to work to earn money to pay for his. I asked what she would do next.

"I'm living with Josh and his family. He moved back in with them. They have cats, Mom. And I watch movies with his brothers."

"Are you helping them? They have to work, you know."

"Oh, of course, I wash the floor when Josh's mom is at work."

"Hmmm." I couldn't imagine her doing that, but I couldn't imagine, nor could I picture, someone putting up with her sitting around while they worked. Albeit, I had for years.

"But I think I'm a burden. I was wondering if I could move in with you and Phil? I could take classes at the university. I'd help you. I know Phil is sick, but I could help. I'd help you clean and get groceries and cook…"

"No, Elizabeth. No. You can't move in with us." I pictured her sitting in my extra bedroom brooding among her mess, of asking her to vacuum and hearing the machine turn off and be put away after five minutes, and of her cooking and leaving everything on the counters and in the sink for days. I explained to her, "You have no idea how sick Phil is and how hard it is. I can't even risk hoping that you'd help us." There was a long pause and then I said, "Thanks for asking, though. Please keep in touch."

"I will. Josh and his family think I should."

Midway through Phil's medical regimen, his appetite waned. He slept more around the clock and his breathing slowed. When he did feel good, he wanted to go out. One Sunday afternoon, we browsed an art fair. There, we met an Oglala woman jeweler and her uncle, who was a wind instrument maker. Phil inquired if they made drums. The woman, Shawna, gave us an email address for her friend.

Phil stuck the paper in his pocket. Two weeks passed and Phil's breathing became worse. The staff at University Hospitals told us the accumulation of medicine in his body would intensify his condition. We shouldn't worry, they said, and then explained that once the treatment stopped, he'd rebound. Studies have shown that if treatment discontinued before six months, the virus could not be annihilated. The virus hadn't been detected in blood tests since late January. From the doctors' views, all proceeded suitably.

At home, when Phil picked up the shirt he'd worn to the art fair, the piece of paper containing the drum-maker's contact fell from the pocket. Phil emailed the man who was a sun dancer, and a few days later a reply arrived saying that he had prayed over an elk skin for direction in the sweat lodge, hoping to use the material to construct a drum for himself, but the answer denied his wishes. After returning to his home, he had found Phil's request. He returned to the sweat lodge and his prayers guided him to make the drum for Phil.

Meanwhile, Phil's breathing worsened. He ate barely anything, subsisting day to day on Jell-O and cottage cheese, and an occasional bite of macaroni and cheese, or soup.

One night I had fixed him three different suppers, trying to find something he might find appealing. On my last trip up the stairs to his bedside, by accident he swung out his hand just as I brought the spoon to his mouth. Jell-O flew, landing on the bed covers. He murmured, "I'm just not hungry."

I cried out, "I can't do this anymore," and ran down the stairs. I wanted to grab the dogs and take them for a long walk, to play with them, to enjoy *something*.

I retreated to the garage, a dark and private place, though chilly in the early spring weather. As I groped for Phil's shop chair, I stepped on the prongs of the fallen garden rake, causing the handle to swing up and hit me between the eyes. I staggered backward, uttered the F-word and stomped my feet. My eyes welled. *Don't take Phil from me. Don't let him die.*

I thought of a friend whose daughter had had cancer. At the time, my friend said she wanted to run away. How easily I could do that, pack my bags, and load the dogs, my patient friends. I could call Mike and Ruth and just say, "I'm not doing this anymore." Leaving would remedy my obsession with death, or so I surmised. I could choose to be alone rather than fall victim to another loved one dying, an angst that shadowed me. If Phil did die, I wouldn't even have to know. In that moment, the idea of escaping seemed fathomable and agreeable. I envisioned it.

The dogs, Sebastian and Ella, also mortals, whined from the other side of the door. What caused their cries now? Did they need something? Did Phil need something?

I rubbed my sore third eye where a lump had arisen. Clearly this mishap carried a message. My reasoning had been temporarily clouded. I knew that nothing is completely easy. How ridiculous to think I could leave Phil. Misery would claim me without him. He had enkindled me, supported me, and loved me.

Our relationship had founded itself after years of repeated chances. How lucky for me to find a blessed love at my age, a man who embodied similar outlooks and feelings as mine. We consistently thought alike. When my injured brain took a hiatus, Phil insisted I use definitive words, a therapy method that has helped to mend my cerebral disabilities. He sees the comic in me, dug the artist out from hiding, and appreciated my sensitivity for children and animals.

Upstairs, Phil lie waiting for help. I would follow him through. He would not die. I would not allow it.

The day after my revelation in the garage, Phil and I spent almost twelve hours in the emergency room. In days following, Phil's breathing worsened because the Internal Medicine staff refused to accept that he truly had lung problems.

During that week, the drum that had been prayed over and created specifically for Phil by the holy man arrived via UPS. Phil used it each day, supined on the couch or on the bed. He set it on his chest and spent what little energy he could lifting its beater for a steady fall. *Ba-bom, ba-bom, ba-bom.* Serenity reverberated throughout the house. It beckoned Raymond's spirit, Phil said. Raymond urged him to live, to play, to enjoy. As a little boy, Raymond used to say he was my angel. Apparently, he knew more than I about other worlds.

In late April, our primary care nurse practitioner referred Phil to a pulmonologist who abruptly removed Phil from the hepatitis remedy, three weeks prior to its scheduled end. The pulmonologist started Phil, under a vigilant watch, on a high dose of prednisone. Phil had pneumonitis, one of only thirty-some recorded cases in the world brought on by the chemotherapy. Another week of the chemotherapy might have closed off his bronchial tubes and ultimately suffocated him.

We had weekly appointments at first with the pulmonologist, who thought Phil might have to be on some dose of prednisone for life. Under the spell of this high-powered drug, Phil sped around the house, organizing kitchen drawers, bookcases, magazines, dresser drawers, all things, whether they needed to be systematized or not. He slept little, working on a house design into the wee hours of the mornings. He talked non-stop. In the days leading up to his change of doctors and clinics, he had dropped nearly fifteen pounds. Now, whatever he consumed his body immediately used.

Emotionally exhausted once again, I drooped, needing a lengthy holiday. I had Phil, though, and I had hope.

Phil continued the drum sessions each day and began to work with an acupuncturist. By summer's end, his resilience surprised everyone. His lungs were recovering, and blood tests still revealed no trace of the C virus. Other complications, however, arose from taking such harsh drugs. He had developed a retinal occlusion, which caused another gruesome treatment. Eventually Phil healed. Each year his blood tests reveal no hepatitis virus. The whites of his eyes are just that—white— and his vision is good.

As for Elizabeth, she has continued to repeat the same behaviors.

I had chosen a green dress to walk with Phil in Mardi Gras, a parade when defenses can be let down, where one can assume the inherent persona. I, a blithely Lady on that day, had reason to celebrate. I had been fortunate to alight on my feet, surviving an accident when I should have been killed. More importantly, I felt honored to have a devoted friend and lover. Nothing is finer than unspoken understanding, the quintessence of a couple. I had dreamt of such rare harmony. It satiates, fills the spirit, and creates no need to want.

Green lives, nourishes, and instills hope, all reasons that I chose green for the dress I made to wed Phil. Evergreen conifers in the dead of winter, green lettuce popping up from tiny seeds, green tops the heat of radishes, and green thyme stimulates breath. Nature encompasses all of these.

Our high, threatened by Phil's health, brought me back to reality: Love didn't promise to be completely carefree. I could say my love for Phil came with the laundry—with the towels blowing on the line. Death, however, could bluster him away, leaving me companionless, though not completely alone.

As the Tibetans say, we *will* live on after death. This I know because I still feel Raymond's presence.

CHAPTER
Ten

SET FREE

"So, Mom. I'm calling to tell you that you and Phil were right. I should have seen a doctor earlier. The testing shows that I have an autoimmune disease. I have to wait for insurance to okay further testing to make sure, but they're thinking that it's lupus."

Elizabeth begins every one of her calls with "So...". Phil says she gets it from me.

My cell phone lays on the table in front of me. I don't like to hold it up to my ear and I also need to do something with my hands when I talk, so I doodle on a piece of note paper. The circles I'm making grow bigger and heavier. "They're certain?" I ask, hoping that the doctors have made a big mistake, yet feeling conflicted. Elizabeth has fabricated illnesses ever since the accident. But then again, she has been tripping and falling for some time and her legs seem to be weakening.

"They think the onset was in my teenage years. It's attacking my nervous system, but it could also be the reason why I've had so many surgeries: ovarian, gall bladder, the troubles in giving birth to Aries. I've always had pain."

"Why didn't you ever tell me that you were in pain?" I click the pen, laying it down in front of me. She has my full attention now. I noticed that her speech has slowed down, something she does before uttering a lie, when she takes longer to think things through before she talks. Even so, I do have to wonder if these infirmities are due to intoxication.

"Because I thought everyone had pain. I thought that was a part of life," she responds.

This kid, a young woman now, has lived a life of pain. Her hell of an early childhood, her brother dying in the car crash, a brain disorder diagnosis of bipolar that probably affected her bad choices. And now this, if it's for real.

One January, a few years ago, when Phil and I first lived in Covington, an obviously distraught Elizabeth called us. She'd been living with a boy and his family who used her to bring in a paycheck for them. She'd gotten pregnant, and feeling frightened, she begged for help. Phil called friends, John and Kelsie, who lived close to where Elizabeth did in Iowa and they immediately responded, going that very day to move her to their home until Phil could drive north and get her. She arrived at our house shortly before her twenty-first birthday, her middle already rounded and protruding.

We rented a small cottage for her, insisted that she get a job and then sat her down to have some serious talks. We told her we'd support whatever she decided, and we also explained to her what taking care of a baby involved, and how expensive having a child would be. She got a one-night-a-week job at a pizza restaurant owned by friends of Phil's. After about three months, she concluded it would be better to give up the baby for adoption. At Lamaze classes, which Phil and I attended with her, she asked about agencies. The instructor gave her a list and she chose Catholic Charities in New Orleans. Of course, these people delighted in knowing that a baby would soon make some couple happy. Elizabeth took this matter seriously. After reading through a folder of applications and thinking about them for several days, she brought them to us, stating that she had chosen three. Would we listen to the applicants' writings and help her make the right selection? However, I believe she'd already made up her mind. After she read them to us, she said her favorite, a couple in their thirties—the man a detective, and the woman, an accountant—seemed the best financially equipped and their values seemed closely related to her own. They also wanted to keep an open adoption, as did she.

Elizabeth insisted upon having a doula help her prepare and to be at her side when she delivered. This woman and I stayed with her through the birthing process and Phil positioned himself down the hall. The baby girl arrived with no complications and in a relatively short time. The following day, the adoptive parents arrived and named the little girl, Emma Rae. The adoptive parents gave the name Rae as an homage to Raymond, Elizabeth's brother.

Vowing to do better, Elizabeth then signed up for fall classes at the University of New Orleans. I helped her pay for school and I helped her buy a car, thinking that perhaps she would now settle and become more serious about her future. We had a deal about the car: she would be the sole driver until we were able to transfer it to her name. One day, I received an official notice in the mail. New Orleans traffic cameras photographed it running a red light in the middle of the night. Elizabeth then admitted that she had been renting it out, one of many clues that our deal was being broken.

She managed well in the first semester, did okay in the second, and had barely begun her third semester when she dropped all the credits after the date that she could receive a tuition refund.

An attorney once offered me unsolicited advice that I could take legal steps to disown Elizabeth, saying that my life would be free without her. What is that? Granted, my life with Elizabeth has been filled with severe ups and downs. Just when I think she's headed on a good path, she explodes and back tracks. But what would she do without someone to turn to? Despite her troubles, she has a tender heart and a bright brain. I continue to believe in her, even though my patience and hope often vacillate and I want to give up.

One morning when Elizabeth still lived in Louisiana, I awakened late. I didn't feel quite right, having a stomach disagreement and some dizziness. Moving from bed quickly in order to get to the toilet before vomiting, a sensation of heaviness in my head tipped me over backward. I blacked out.

When Phil leaned over, asking me to please come to, my eyes couldn't focus, nor did they want to stay open. I had a nasty headache. I failed at an attempt to sit. Phil helped me scoot back into the shower and he turned on the cold water. In and out of consciousness I wavered, trying hard to focus, trying hard to stay with the present when what I wanted to do was slouch down and let go, let the blackness engulf me. Phil, however, wouldn't hear of it. After some time (Phil later said maybe 10 minutes had elapsed), my vision improved, and I became aware of my surroundings. I don't really remember being dried off or being dressed, although I do remember walking down the outside steps to the car. Two people helped me, one by each arm, and Elizabeth, who happened to be there, hung onto my shirt from the back. After many medical tests and having the back of my head stapled, the ER workers allowed me to go home. They did not know, however, that the metencephalon part of my midbrain, which controls a person's equilibrium and sense of space among other abilities, had been affected. I would find that out much later. At home, I rested for three days and then gradually began my routines, including swimming, and walking two miles a day. I felt fine, at least for some time.

A little more than two years after Elizabeth had moved to be with us, she arrived at the house one day and told me she would return to Iowa. This time she planned to live with a fellow she'd known in high school. I also knew him, and I knew that he had married and had children. His parents were known to have been alcoholics. Elizabeth insisted he had not married, and he did not have any children because he'd told her so. When she arrived in Iowa, she promptly gave him control of the money she'd been given from the compensation for our accident. He spent all of it, all meaning a lot of money.

I have to stop and think about what went on in my younger mind. Did I do senseless things? Yes. Did I give money away? No. I didn't have it to give. Did I listen to my parents' common sense? Sometimes I did, though rarely when it came to crushes on men. My family, however, had instilled values in me that did call for sound judgment and mostly I followed that guidance.

I fretted that I'd not done enough as a mother to teach Elizabeth to think reasonably, but I assured myself that she would learn and come to her senses about the guy. Instead, she stayed with him for five years and for most of that time, she cut off communication with me and Phil.

After all we'd done for her. The very words I never wanted to hear myself say hung over me like a dirt cloud. When I'd heard that phrase uttered by others, it sounded to me as though the offspring were indebted to repay the parents. But now I said it, "After all we'd done for her."

For weeks after she left Louisiana for a life with a guy whom I knew to be less than stable, my nights filled with tossing and turning. My chest felt as though my main artery had been drained of blood.

My friends and now in-laws, Mike and Ruth, called periodically to relay the gossip about Elizabeth and her beau: They had bought a new truck. He had bought guns. Every time Mike and Ruth called, they disclosed something else that stretched my nerves like a too-taut violin string. Finally, I insisted that they not tell me anything more about her, not ever. If she refused to communicate with us, I couldn't stand hearing about her second and third hand.

What parent can tolerate seeing their child deny the ideals that we've taught them? Elizabeth is not my biological daughter, yet long ago she had become a part of me. Knowing her and caring about her during her early years brought me to love her as deeply as anyone can love a child.

In the beginning of her relationship with this man, Elizabeth may have cut off communication with us. As time went on, he made sure she didn't interact with anyone but his family and friends. My sister, though, became acquainted with a family that were friends of the fellow and in this way, Sis kept tabs on Elizabeth.

Then I heard through Mike and Ruth that Elizabeth had given birth to a little girl and named her Arianna. Something inside of me turned sour. I literally retched, and my hands shook. Why by him? What did I do to turn her away from us, and especially from me? I told Mike and Ruth, again, that I did not want to hear about Elizabeth. She had chosen her life and it was her business. I told my sister, who always seems to know somebody who knows the person of interest, the same thing. Sis gets her information the Irish way, my father once said, meaning that she never asks straightforward questions, rather she asks trick questions, ones that skirt the issue, but gets the information she seeks. I wanted to hear Elizabeth's information from Elizabeth and not through the grapevine.

One day Ruth broke that rule and called to tell me I should know that Elizabeth and the baby had gone away with the father. No one knew where.

I started drinking wine every night, and not just one glass. One January night, I tripped on the outside brick steps and caught myself with my arms. Even under the influence, my arms had immediate excruciating pain. By morning, I couldn't move either shoulder without wincing. For weeks, I wouldn't be able to sleep on either side. Winter in Louisiana may be attractive compared to snow covered months elsewhere, but the chilled humidity gets into the bones. I craved heat on my upper back and arms. But instead of making a doctor's appointment, I wished the pain away. It didn't work.

One morning in the very wee hours, I awoke to lights having been turned on. I heard Phil in the bathroom groaning and I found him in a tub filled with hot water, his pallor gray. He begged me to call the ambulance and when I found my phone, I shook so hard that I could barely push the numbers. Phil had his gall bladder removed that night and while I sat with him, watching the hustle around the emergency room, I vowed to stop drinking. I did not want to end up in an ER ever again.

Five weeks later, after Phil healed and returned to his routines, my sister wrote me a note. Elizabeth and family had returned to Iowa. Shortly after that, I found myself swaying when I walked, not having total control over my legs. I could no longer walk our dogs, Ella and Sebastian, as I never quite knew where my feet were. Sebastian had become a therapy dog with the Visiting Pet Program in New Orleans. He and I had been working nursing homes twice a month. Soon after the disequilibrium set in, we had to quit; I tripped over everything including my own feet. I went to doctors and not one helped. The summer passed. I did not receive any word directly from Elizabeth. My symptoms worsened.

I now know that nerves run throughout our body and connect to the brain. My brain had been badly injured, as had my nervous system. Therefore, the relationship of my body, mind and spirit suffered. My care and concerns for Elizabeth most likely also provoked my nerves to misfire, causing pain and other symptoms, such as dizziness and imbalance.

That October, little Ella dog turned twelve and a half years old. She had been failing for some time. I couldn't even bend over or sit on the floor to hold and pet her. Tears rolled out of my eyes as much out of frustration as of sorrow. Ella died the day before Elizabeth's daughter Arianna's first birthday.

My sister wrote me another note. She and her daughter and son had gone to Arianna's party. When they told Elizabeth, who had picked Ella out of a litter of puppies, that she had died, Elizabeth cried. Hearing this gave me hope that she still carried some sense of "home" in her heart.

Sis commented that the family Elizabeth had involved herself with "were different." Nevertheless, my sister had been pleased with the invitation. My niece gave me another report: Elizabeth's beau had done nothing but talk of bar fights and shooting guns, completely oblivious that he had ruined any chances of gaining my niece's approval.

My condition worsened and then, in March 2017, three and a half years after Elizabeth had moved from Louisiana, Mike and Ruth called to inform us that Ruth had pancreatic cancer. About the same time, my sister wrote another note telling me that Elizabeth had again given birth, but with complications. She and the baby boy, Aries, stayed in the hospital with Aries confined to an incubator. Elizabeth's gall bladder burst shortly before the birth, which caused sepsis. Despite her critical condition, neither Elizabeth's boyfriend, nor his parents had bothered to call me. This made me certain that she wanted no contact.

Meanwhile, I had a bad feeling that the political climate, as well as the weather, in Louisiana was impacting my health. With my insistence, Phil and I made plans to go to Santa Fe for one week to house hunt. Then we planned to drive to Iowa to say our goodbyes to Ruth. The New Mexico part of the trip could have been put on hold for another time. However, without mentioning it to each other, it became a way to procrastinate. Neither of us wanted to bid our farewells to Ruth.

We had no expectations to find a house on our first week in Santa Fe, but we did. Immediately, we began the process to get a loan and make the purchase. New Mexico's never-ending blue sky and cumulous clouds, arid earth, and sacred mountains promised healing.

By the time we arrived in Iowa, crocuses and daffodils bloomed and trees were greening. Farmers were planting corn and soybeans. Ruth's yard, which she had carefully tended with flowers for thirty years, began to push up from the earth and bloom. I wanted to hug Ruth, but both of us feared I might topple over on her. She had always been several inches shorter than me and now she was thin and frail. I couldn't move without stumbling, like a toy whose feet stay in one place on its pedestal, but the figure leans this way and that, wherever someone's fingers want to direct them from underneath the base.

While there, once again I wanted to search for Elizabeth, to tell her that I missed her, but fatigue overwhelmed the urge. No matter how much sleep I got, I had no energy. I didn't know it at that time, but the lack of stamina had been complicated by heavy medications that an ear surgeon had prescribed.

Back in Louisiana, the surgeon convinced me that an incision of the inner ear was the only solution to my imbalance and other issues. I scheduled it for June. Ruth passed away three days before I went on the table. I couldn't seem to comprehend that she, a friend for thirty-some years, no longer existed. She had been a friend to Elizabeth, too, and Ruth had listened to my woes all those years about raising Elizabeth. Now, I had to put her on a shelf in my thoughts to retrieve later. My own physical woes became foremost. After the surgery the same sensations, and more, plagued me whether I sat, stood, walked, or laid down. The feeling of a momentary blackout when walking worsened.

At the end of the summer, Phil and I made our move to Santa Fe, and then in November, we traveled to Wisconsin to have our traditional Thanksgiving dinner with my side of the family.

In Iowa, we stayed with Mike, who, without Ruth, had his own misery. Elizabeth had been kind to contact Mike and he invited her family to visit so that we could meet the children. With Arianna, two years old, and Aries at six months, Elizabeth was planning her wedding. I could not find any joy in her intention, as I wondered if the fellow had gotten a divorce from his wife. I observed, as well, that Elizabeth didn't seem excited. I wrestled with calling him Elizabeth's boyfriend. I didn't want to accept him as so, but he was the children's biological father and by this time they had been together for four years.

The guy seemed to think that he needed to impress us, as he had my niece at Arianna's birthday. He talked bar fights and weapons, which we found difficult to comment on. I had decided to keep quiet; it wasn't my life. When they left, Elizabeth promised to keep in touch, and this time she did.

November in Iowa casts a loneliness with the cold, the trees bared of leaves, the sky gray and overcast. The mood of the atmosphere seemed appropriate for the despair I sensed for and in Elizabeth and her situation. I felt awful in general. The surgery had only made imbalance and dizziness worse for me. I continued to grip a cane with a clenched fist, the same type of force that seemed to enshroud Elizabeth's life.

The following March, Elizabeth flew on her own to visit us. During her two-day stay, Phil and I both prompted her to leave him. We told her that she is much smarter than he and that she deserved better.

"The clock is ticking away," I said, "and I want you to understand that Phil and I are behind you. During my first marriage, no one ever said to me that this life is yours, not his."

She told us that she had already been contemplating this. When she returned to her home, she gathered up the children and left him. She had nowhere to go, though, except to the home of his best friend, who has several children of his own. Even so, he and his wife took in Elizabeth, Arianna, and Aries, and tried to keep the children's biological father from contact. But after three weeks, he barged into the house and convinced Elizabeth he would change.

"I'm sorry, Mom, but I had to go back with him. He promised me it'd be different."

What could I say? I knew he wouldn't change. But she had to find this out for herself.

Phil began to make more periodic trips to Iowa to help Mike, who planned to move to Santa Fe to be closer to us. As Phil readied for one trip, I gathered some of Elizabeth's things that we still had. Once in Iowa, Phil went to the address we had for her in a small town. The place appeared empty. Boxes and bags of trash lay strewn about both inside and on the porch, along with a baby stroller. Even so, he deposited what he had brought for Elizabeth there.

When Elizabeth returned to gather the last few things in their move, she found what Phil had left. Since she did not have a phone of her own, she had to wait to use the boyfriend's cell phone, whereupon she called Mike, surmising that Phil would be there.

Elizabeth and family were moving to a mobile home in the countryside. She had no phone and no vehicle unless the boyfriend was home. They had no near neighbors. This led me to more worry. Had she been so brainwashed that she had no thoughts of normalcy, of tending to her children's and her own needs? I began to wonder if these people were the type upon whom horror novels are based. To help, in what small way we could, we added her to our cell phone plan.

After that, however, Elizabeth began to check in with us more regularly. She told us that she would be having ovarian surgery, but it hadn't been scheduled as she had no help with the children. Suddenly she stopped calling.

Almost a year after Phil had left Elizabeth's belongings on her porch, Phil prepared for another trip to Iowa to help Mike. I asked Phil to please find Elizabeth, spend some time with her, perhaps take her to lunch. My intuition nagged me, and I felt we needed to try again to convince her, somehow, to leave there and begin a new life.

The day that Elizabeth had been legally adopted, I promised to always look after her, a vow that I took in earnest and still would not allow my conscience to abandon; I was apprehensive that she hadn't yet reached a point where she could conduct her life maturely. And now she had little ones to consider. I began to wonder if she had a mental handicap. Perhaps she didn't have the capability to think logically.

In Iowa again, Phil invited Elizabeth to breakfast with him. When they met, she jumped in his truck. Before he could say a word, she told him she'd had it, and she needed out. She'd pack the van, which was in her name, and drive it to Santa Fe. Phil took one look at the van and took it to a repair shop, and then straight to the junkyard. We rented a car for Elizabeth and told her to gather the kids and go straight to the women's shelter. She did.

As soon as Phil returned home, I packed my car and drove to Iowa to bring Elizabeth to Santa Fe. Once there, we had to wait for the children to have the last appointment with their pediatrician. Their behavior exhausted me. Constantly angry and crying, they refused to listen to instructions. I felt I'd already paid my dues in life, having dealt with this behavior for so many years with Elizabeth in her childhood. I was another change in their lives, another instability, basically, someone they did not know.

After two days of this, Arianna and Aries began to settle down, but when we pulled into the parking lot at the doctor's office, the other grandmother appeared, opened Arianna's door, and grabbed her. Hysterically, the woman jabbered over and over how she would miss the children and how could we take them from her. She carried them into the doctor's appointment, gave them each a bag of coloring books, cheap plastic toys, and lots of sugar-coated candy, all of which smelled like cigarette smoke. She did not look at me nor did she acknowledge me.

After a bit, I asked her why she couldn't say, "Hello."

She replied, "Elizabeth said you wouldn't want to talk to me." Had Elizabeth told her this to save me from being hassled, or to hide things that she herself had said and done? The whole situation had bubbled up. Now I felt doubtful about Elizabeth's integrity. I began to wonder if I'd gotten myself on another roller coaster ride in her world.

When a nurse showed Elizabeth and the kids to a room, the grandmother barged in, too, only to leave a few minutes later. Shortly after, Elizabeth appeared, asking me to come in because the kids needed a grandmother, one that wouldn't make them scream.

Before that day, I had empathized with the other grandmother. Afterward, I hoped I wouldn't see her or hear from her again. After our long trek back, however, she began to call, crying into the phone that we'd taken her children away. Each time Phil told her not to call again. I refused to talk with her. Eventually we had to change our phone numbers. My response may be considered mean, but Elizabeth and the children were staying with us. Their room looked like a tornado hit it. Elizabeth cried or had consistent temper tantrums, as did Arianna. Aries threw food, toys, and everything he touched. Phil's and my nerves were on edge from all that chaos.

After three weeks, we moved Elizabeth and the children to an apartment, which we paid for. After a year, we bought a house for them with a promise from Elizabeth that she would keep it clean or be evicted. It has never been easy to move her. She has no idea how to pack, nor will she try. She has no notion of what it means to organize, to fold clothes, to pack kitchen supplies, or to keep anything clean. When we moved her from the apartment to the house, she didn't help and all of their belongings were dirty. Nevertheless, we hoped for the best, knowing that we were doing it for the children, who needed space to play and, as they grew older, to study.

Meanwhile, Elizabeth stated that the children's biological father had done nothing to stay in contact and paid no child support. Apparently, he had still not divorced his wife, but shortly after Elizabeth's departure, he had another woman with children move in with him.

My health has improved slowly. Alternative medicines are plentiful here in New Mexico where an ancient spirituality emits a healing that doesn't exist in other places I have been.

I think about these past years since Elizabeth left Louisiana as she tells me about her most recent diagnosis. I can relate to her feelings, our symptoms being similar in many ways. The crux of our pain, however, stems from different etiologies. My pain has stemmed from environmental issues, or the many accidents which have happened. On the other hand, we have learned that autoimmune diseases are genetic, as is bipolar disorder. The practice of finding new parents for children who have come from less than desirable homes includes destroying their biological family records, thus also ridding them of their medical history. Had I known in Elizabeth's adolescent years the possibilities of an autoimmune and bipolar disorder, these conditions probably could have been caught. She could have had medical help much earlier than at thirty years old. And if she truly does have an autoimmune disease, treatment at a younger age could have prevented further muscle and nerve weakening. Medication for the bipolar disorder may have lessened her bizarre behaviors. As a teenager, she perfected hiding these behaviors from therapists and psychiatrists, displaying them only to me, which makes me wonder if her diagnosis really is correct. Even though I suspected she might be bipolar, no professional would take that into consideration. I had asked doctors and therapists if she could possibly be psychotic because of her sudden mood changes, with severe highs and lows, and risk-taking, all characteristics of the disorder. At that time, professionals were reluctant to label her due to her young age.

My attention returns to our conversation about her most recent analysis. Why is it that some have such heaviness dumped on them? Elizabeth had a nasty early childhood and lost her brother when she was only twelve. A brain disorder led her to involve herself with people who used her, and that interfered with her ability to set goals. She has had lifelong emotional pain.

She handles this news better than I do, better than I would, if it were my diagnosis. But then there is a part of me that wonders if she is making up the autoimmune disease. She has a reputation of being manipulative and of lying. I do want, however, to give her the benefit of the doubt, so I mention that she has matured. She reminds me that if medication didn't work for the bipolar disorder, she wouldn't be doing very well.

In the beginning, Phil and I had some strong doubts about bringing Elizabeth and the children here to be close to us. Elizabeth spiraled downward after she had been in New Mexico for only a few months. Her first address, the apartment, turned into a pigsty and she indulged in alcohol. I tried to get her to understand that she could have her children removed if she didn't get out of bed, take them to school and daycare and keep their environment clean, but I failed. That is, she ignored my advice until someone else reported her and the children were almost taken away. Fortunately, the social worker sent the children to Phil and me until Elizabeth cleaned the apartment. Somehow Elizabeth doesn't understand that children need a hygienic environment.

"Mom, I really think I need to see someone, talk to someone, because I am not doing well," she said to me one day. This was after Ruth's death, after her Aunt Joan, who had been a support to her during her teen years, had passed away, and shortly after that a dear friend of hers went missing. (His body would be found several months later.)

Elizabeth did her research and found a psychiatrist and a therapist, both of whom she kept working with for at least two years. Her therapist not only worked with Elizabeth's needs, but also guided her in raising her children. She learned to be consistent in taking prescribed pills because she wanted to raise her children. Elizabeth used all possible resources to get Arianna and Aries in good daycare and good schools. As a result, the children became a delight to be with. Elizabeth also told me that she is taking classes to become a veterinary technician, something she continually said that she yearned to pursue. I wanted to believe this, although after enrolling in five different colleges over the years, and her escape-from-academics techniques, I remain dubious. Now at 31 years old, I still hope that she can find an occupation that will please her.

She says she's a work in progress.

Several months later, Phil and I are standing with Elizabeth outside of the house that we bought for her and the children. Elizabeth is without her children, as she has permanently lost custody. She does not look good. She appears to not have slept for a while, her hair sticks out in all directions and her bare feet are coated with something black and sticky. She says it is because she is cleaning, though she is not, and she has not. For the past year, she has been telling us that she is scrubbing floors, washing cupboards, sweeping under furniture, in other words keeping a tidy house. She has not let us in the house very often and when we have seen it, we considered it a growing health hazard and unsafe for anyone to live in due to the filth. For several months, we have been insisting that she scour her home. The children do not deserve to live in such vile conditions. But she doesn't like us to tell her what needs to be done and gets irritated every time we say anything.

Phil and I had driven to a family wedding a thousand miles from here. While we were still out of state, a policeman called us. He had found the children playing in a street far from their home. When he brought them to their house, he found deplorable conditions and called in Child Services. The children were sent to live with their biological father in Iowa, and by Iowa law, Phil and I have no grandparental rights, so we may not ever get to see them again.

When we finally see the inside of the house, it stinks like a trash can that has been sitting and festering for months. House and fruit flies abound, as do black widow spiders. Elizabeth never threw out anything. We are devastated to see the disaster, and I feel like an idiot for trusting that her behavior could change.

A few days later, she is gone, and she lied to us about her method of leaving. In our last face-to-face conversation with her, she said that we should not have to clean up her mess. Yet she fled and gave no forwarding address or phone number. Her fabrication of hygienics and of her world being in good order sinks into both of us. Perhaps she planned this loss of her children in order to rid herself of the responsibility of caring for them, whether or not that was conscious on her part. In doing this, she freed herself to live with yet another boyfriend in another state.

I feel as though I have filled Phil's life with troubles and worries that came about because of Elizabeth's mental and my physical instabilities. By choosing to be Elizabeth's mother, I have carried her burden. Phil chose to help me carry this load and I could not have done it without him. Sometimes it has caused a heaviness in our relationship. Now though, except for heartache about the children, we have given ourselves permission to let go of Elizabeth. This latest abandonment makes us realize that she is mentally unstable, and no matter what we might do, we cannot get through to her, and we no longer have the desire nor the energy to try. Help must come from inside herself.

People have asked me over the years, each time after Elizabeth disappeared, why I gave up on her. The truth is that I did not; it was Elizabeth who left and forfeited communication. It's her pattern to make a mess and escape. This time she has made her largest mess yet, leaving us with the cleanup. The suffering that she has caused her children is sacrilegious. How she left the condition of the house is inexcusable.

Phil put substantial efforts into making this structure a home for Elizabeth and the children. Most importantly, he gave them things that he built with his hands and his tools, and they were destroyed. I was foolish enough to believe that her consistently using people was a matter of needing to mature, and maybe of facing her early childhood demons. I feel, now, as though I have evolved, that suddenly the truth of the real Elizabeth has appeared. Seeing Phil hurt and taken for granted helped to awaken me. From here, we will carry a profound grief for the grandchildren. At the same time, letting go of their mother allows a lightness to return to our lives.

Epilogue

*"I've looked at life from both sides now
From win and lose and still somehow
It's life's illusions I recall
I really don't know life at all."*
Joni Mitchell

I talk to Raymond every day. I ask him how he likes a painting I am working on. I tell him about our animal friends, and on the rare occasion when I sit down to play my piano, I play one of the songs that he once played. I will always wonder what he would be like as an adult and I will forever miss him.

Due to Phillip's devoted nature, he has backed me in every episode with Elizabeth from the time she graduated from high school. He has bolstered me through the deaths of friends and family members. He has been ten steps ahead of me in everything that needs to be done from yard labor, to cooking, to house chores, even hanging towels on the line. He builds frames for my artwork and does other things that he does not have to. He has stood beside me when I have needed a crutch for my physical and emotional challenges, both concerns that with his help are slowly healing and I think about them less each day.

I am gaining better health all the time. I have lived with equilibrium issues for so long now that I can detect if it is caused by an inner ear malfunction, vertebral defects, or compounded ailments. I adjust my daily routine by how my body decides to function on that specific day. In spite of what discomfort or pain I may feel, I have found that the important elements in my life are friends—animals and humans—and standing up for their respective rights.

Sometimes I still long for my place in the country with the horses and the sheep. Then I realize that if I had to make a choice between Phillip and that life again, I would prefer this path. Before I landed in this mental and emotional realm where I am presently, my endeavors were many. Every one of those experiences has contributed to my mental and spiritual growth. I am now sturdy within myself. With Phillip, I can share my passions for reading, writing, art, and music. He cherishes our animal friends as much as I do, a trait that is most important to me. My epoch with Phillip is where I am meant to be. After all of these years, my heart feels complete.

Acknowledgments

This project would not have moved forward if it were not for the encouragement of the writing group that I have worked with for over thirty years. I bow to Sharon Hanson, Patrick Irelan, Coleen Maddy, and David Ricketts for plodding through the early stages of these essays, and for listening to my sad stories and wading through my tears after the accident.

I am beholden to Ann McCutchan for her intuitive editing skills and advice. She took the manuscript in its raw and guided me. My gratitude goes out to BK Loren, Elizabeth Stuckey-French and Ned Stuckey-French for consistently encouraging my writing over the years.

Thank you to the Pen Women Press, especially Lucy Arnold, Managing Editor, for her excellent direction in putting this book together and transferring my illustrations into an attractive cover. And, to Julie Arnold for her diligent proofreading. Thank you to Christine Baker for her expertise in design and layout.

I also express my utmost appreciation to my sister, Mary Flaherty, for reminding me that I need to write, and to her and my niece, Molly Flaherty, for their care and harboring of Elizabeth and me, and for Molly's expert veterinarian advice concerning my animals. To my brother Michael Hart and his wife, Joan Hart, for giving me the use of their acreage in Wisconsin so that I could write solely and without interruption for a week. If I needed to talk, needed a break, needed help with Elizabeth, they propped me up over a number of years. I am eternally grateful for their emotional support.

The days, months, and years after the accident would have been unbearable without the friendship and heartfelt support of those I have mentioned above and of the following people: Mike and Ruth Kehoe, for always coming to help when I called, for advising me, and for helping with my gardens; Jim and Rosalie Cahill for consistently offering their help; Mike and Sheila Dalton for listening and calming my nerves with Manhattans and helping me with the acreage; and Peggy Timm, Barb Burke, and my sister-in-law, Joan, for staying with me in the weeks after my release from the hospital to help with Elizabeth and the critters. Everything would have fallen apart without their aide. Rebecca Crutchfield and Alan Stoker for doing everything and more that longtime friends do for each other; Gwen and Ying Ying for encouraging Elizabeth to continue playing her violin and to listen to me, not to mention the delicious Chinese meals that Ying cooked; Mary and Dan Buol, Merle and Bill Eggert, Margaret Bailey and Dan Miller and Nate, Eden Hall, and Amy Lynch for being the best neighbors and friends that anyone could ever ask for; Dr. Alan and Claudia Beyer for the caring, expert veterinarian service and for going an extra mile when my brain didn't function and my body was too broken; Jane Cadwallader for helping me to relearn playing the piano; Matt Jacobson for his expert meticulous legal help; and Lynhon and Dave Stout for their excellent advice and friendship. Thank you to Lucinda Harms, Jan Jacobson, and John and Kelcie Warren for helping with Elizabeth. A special appreciation to Father Ed O'Melia for his spiritual counsel. I will forever appreciate Emily Patton, Nurse Practitioner, for her devoted attention to both Phillip and me. A million thanks to Dr. Peter Fisk, Integrative Chiropractor, for his honest knowledge of the nervous system, and guidance on the road to recovery. And, to my trustworthy friend, Vicki Kurtz Duncan, I give ten million thanks for helping me with everything throughout many years.

Several of the persons I have mentioned have passed on to the next life since I began this endeavor. I miss them immensely. However, I look forward to dancing with them when the veil lifts.

My animal friends who comforted me and gave me reason to laugh, and who have gone before me: Isis, Demetra, Sasha, Jumpin' Jack Flash, Miss Ella, Sebastian, Maile, Kimo, Grrretta, Sassy, and Max. I will always carry them in my heart, and I hope to race with them and with Raymond in an evening dew of the future. And to the present household: Yuka, Hart, and Sol, who put up with me and give me never-ending love. I am grateful for their presence.

I extend my full appreciation to Phillip Kehoe for helping me write "Sunflower, a Poem for Raymond." And most of all I bestow utmost gratitude to Phillip, my love, for helping me with endless readings and edits of this manuscript. But mostly for inspiring my creativity and making my life worth living.

Author's Note

In our country we have abandoned mental health care. People who have brain disorders truly need understanding from loved ones. Family and friends also need support and education in navigating the chaos that mental illness creates. Those of us who are devoted to and interact with people who have psychoses have our own desperations. I strongly support NAMI (National Alliance on Mental Illness), a grassroots organization based in Arlington, Virginia. Every state has organizations and affiliates. More information can be found at NAMI.org. Please consider supporting them.

About the Author

JACINTA HART KEHOE

Jacinta Hart Kehoe began writing as a child by recording her pony's journal and writing short stories. She also drew and painted prolifically. As a young adult, writing non-fiction became her primary course of creativity. She has a Master of Arts degree in English from Bread Loaf School of English, Middlebury, Vermont, and has worked as a high school English and drama teacher, an editor, a waitress, a secretary, a dog trainer, a seamstress, a community organizer, and as a specialist for Iowa Foster and Adoptive Parents Association, among other organizations—all in which editing and writing were her main focus. She has published in various outlets on numerous topics. She began avidly writing creative non-fiction essays about healing after she suffered multiple injuries in a semi-trailer truck/auto accident when her first husband and son were killed. For 19 years, she has needed to periodically attend physical therapy sessions due to vertigo and the need to maintain her equilibrium, results of the accident.

Hart Kehoe gardens, paints, writes, and loves to hike. In 2017, Hart Kehoe and her husband, Phillip—the love of her life—moved to Santa Fe, New Mexico, where they met and adopted special friends Yuka, Hart, and Sol—a dog and two cats.

Website: jchartart.square.site

Works Cited

Ginsburg, Allen. "Sunflower Sutra." In *Howl*. San Francisco: City Lights Books, 1959.

Hoagland, Edward. "Hailing the Elusory Mountain Lion." In *Walking the Dead Diamond River*. New York: Random House, 1973.

Lahr, John. "Waving and Drowning." In *Tennessee Williams: Mad Pilgrimage of the Flesh*. New York: W.W. Norton & Company, Inc., 2014.

Lamott, Anne. *Operating Instructions: A Journal of My Son's First Year*. New York: Pantheon Books, 1993.

Lysaght, Patricia. *The Banshee, the Irish Death Messenger*. Boulder, CO: Roberts Rinehart Publishers, 1997.

Mitchell, Joni. "Both Sides Now." On *Clouds*. A&M Studio, Hollywood: Reprise Records, 1969.

Moss, Robert. *The Dreamer's Book of the Dead: A Soul Traveler's Guide to Death, Dying and the Other Side.* Rochester, Vermont: Destiny Books, 2005.

Rinpoche, Sogyal. *The Tibetan Book of Living and Dying.* Edited by Patrick Gaffney and Andrew Harvey. Harper: San Francisco, 2002.

Sams, Jamie, and Carson, David. *Medicine Cards: The Discovery of Power through the Ways of Animals.* Bear & Co. Publishers: Santa Fe, 1988.

Poem: "Sunflower (for Raymond)," by Jacinta Hart Kehoe and Phillip Kehoe.

CPSIA information can be obtained
at www.ICGtesting.com
Printed in the USA
LVHW040039230623
750504LV00004B/654